THE
ROYAL
WEDDING
DRESSES

THE
ROYAL
WEDDING
DRESSES

NIGEL ARCH AND
JOANNA MARSCHNER

SIDGWICK & JACKSON

LONDON

First published in 1990 by Sidgwick & Jackson Limited

Copyright © 1990 by Nigel Arch and Joanna
Marschner

ISBN 0 283 99860 1

Picture research by Anne Marie Ehrlich
Design by Stevens Design Associates
Layout and typography by Kevin Patrick Cox
Typeset by Rowland Phototypesetting Limited
Bury St Edmunds, Suffolk
Printed by Butler and Tanner Limited
Frome, Somerset
for Sidgwick & Jackson Limited
1 Tavistock Chambers, Bloomsbury Way
London WC1A 2SG

PUBLISHER'S NOTE

The caption for the sketch on the bottom of the
thirteenth page of the colour section is incorrect.
The dress is in fact the one worn by the Tsarina of
Russia, mother of the Grand Duchess Marie of
Russia, at her daughter's wedding to Prince Albert
in 1874. Sketch by Chevalier reproduced by
gracious permission of Her Majesty the Queen.

Nigel Arch dedicates this book to
the memory of his father, Bernard Frank Arch

Joanna Marschner dedicates this book to
her goddaughter, Catherine Mitchell

The shoes worn by HRH The Princess of Wales, on her wedding day. Made by Clive Shilton, they are of ivory silk with mother-of-pearl sequins. (Syndication International)

CONTENTS

INTRODUCTION

OPPOSITE PAGE: *Detail of the beaded embroidery, showing the bee motif on the dress of HRH The Duchess of York. The motif was derived from the Ferguson family crest – a thistle attended by three bumble bees. The sleeves of the dress also carried this motif, as did the train. (HRH The Duchess of York)*

BELOW: *This sad Spanish Princess was married both to Arthur, Prince of Wales, and his brother, Henry VIII. It was her divorce from Henry that led to the split from the Catholic .church. Oil painting by M. Sittow. (National Portrait Gallery)*

ON a fine summer day in 1986, the wedding of the year was celebrated. Prince Andrew, second son of Queen Elizabeth II of Great Britain and Northern Ireland, married Sarah Ferguson, daughter of an officer in Her Majesty's Life Guards. Worldwide, some five hundred million people watched the ceremony on television. Their attention was rewarded by a splendid example of British ceremonial as Miss Ferguson became the Duchess of York.

For the majority of those who watched on television or strained to catch a glimpse of the bride as she drove to Westminster Abbey in the Glass Coach, the most intriguing question that awaited answer was the style of the dress chosen by the bride for the occasion. Literally, traditionally and metaphorically the dress worn by both bride and groom is the central focus of royal weddings.

This book takes a close look at royal wedding dress over five centuries. From this viewpoint, a door is unlocked to reveal the social and political aspects of royal weddings since the reign of King Henry VII, the first Tudor monarch. And it is in these early weddings that the chief protagonists – bride and groom – seem at times to be mere pieces in a greater political game.

Henry's marriage was designed to consolidate a tentative hold on the throne and the marital unions he negotiated for his children were to be extensions of his power base. Romance, within the modern meaning of the term, had no place in Henry's vocabulary – or his world. After the death of his wife he even contemplated marriage with a child who was eventually betrothed to his eldest son Arthur.

If this traditional attitude to matrimony seems very alien to observers in the late twentieth century, Henry, like his successors on the throne, realized the importance of organizing the occasion in the appropriate manner. He spent lavishly for his own wedding, dressing his bride in silk damask and crimson satin. Indeed, costly display appears paramount in accounts of royal weddings.

Until comparatively recently, there was an understanding that the marriage was to serve the dynastic needs of the kingdom, securing the line of succession and extending alliances with other European states. This overrode any concern to ensure the mutual attraction of each of the parties.

Many brides were forced to sail not only these seas of diplomacy, but literally across the North Sea and English Channel as they made their perilous journeys to London. Catherine of Aragon, bride successively of Arthur, Prince of Wales, and Henry VIII, tooks weeks to find her way from Spain to England. Charlotte of Mecklenburg-Strelitz, from her obscure German principality was another storm tossed lover who, at the end of her journey, was horrified to learn that instead of the anticipated period of rest and recuperation, her marriage to King George III was to take place as soon as she arrived in the capital.

Not all the journeys described in this book ended happily. In 1795 travelling hopefully was certainly better than arriving for Caroline of Brunswick, bride of the Prince of Wales. Their first encounter drove the Prince to the brandy bottle, and Caroline to make unkind, if perceptive, pronouncements on her fiancé's size and physiognomy.

There are numerous other surprising marital accounts. Queen Victoria, for example, followed strict protocol by proposing to Prince Albert. Tra-

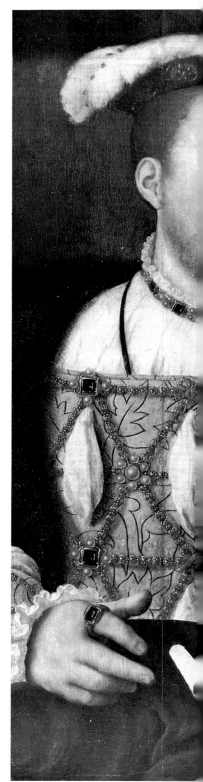

other family members. When speedier methods of communication blossom, so too do our sources. Lengthy coverage in newspapers and magazines extends in the twentieth century to radio and television.

THE story begins five hundred years ago in London on 18 January 1486, with a display of pomp and circumstance. Henry Tudor married Elizabeth of York, eldest daughter and heiress of King Edward IV. Henry, victor of the Battle of Bosworth, which ended the years of civil strife known as the Wars of the Roses, spent lavishly on the wedding. Indeed, in some ways it was a more elaborate occasion than the Coronation. His own gown, of cloth of gold, cost £53 4s 8d and his Queen's, of 'silk damask and crimson satin' £11 5s 6d. As a token of the union of the Royal Houses of York and Lancaster, Henry carried in his hand 'that fair posie wherein the white roses were first tied together'.

Henry's eldest son Arthur, Prince of Wales, was married five times to Catherine of Aragon. Henry VII needed to bolster his power against enemies abroad and this union with a Spanish princess was seen as a key to diplomatic success. As the negotiations between the respective fathers waxed and waned Arthur was married a total of four times by proxy. Eventually, when Prince Arthur was fifteen, the young couple finally met. After considerable delays while the details of the dowry were settled, the Princess eventually left for England in September 1501, arriving in Plymouth in November. She spent the last night of her maidenhood in the Bishop of London's palace. On Sunday 14 November, she rode through the City of London to St Paul's, observing on her way according to *Hall's Chronicle*, 'seven beautiful pageants erected and set up in diverse parts' and hearing 'sweet harmony which sounded with heavenly noise in every side of the street'.

The citizens were in 'fine engrained clothes [and] costly furs', as they watched the procession 'standing upon scaffolds railed from Gracechurch to St Paul's'. In every street there hung 'rich arras, costly tapestry and fine cloths of silver and gold, curious velvets and satins and pleasant silks'. Wine flowed

dition, however, dictated that her dress and its spectacular lace were entirely of British manufacture, as were those of later royal brides including Princess May of Teck. Princess May's dress was worked with a design of flowers 'typical of Britain and Ireland tied with a lover's knot'. This use of symbols was echoed in the dress of the most recent Duchess of York, where bees, derived from Miss Ferguson's family crest, were intermingled with the fouled anchor, an emblem of the Royal Navy, in which service Prince Andrew is an officer.

This book is about dress history and social history – the two are inevitably intertwined. The story emerges from a myriad of sources. Early background to the weddings is to be found in the pages of the *Calendar of State Papers* and the negotiations between England and Spain over the marriage between Arthur, Prince of Wales, and Catherine of Aragon. Later we have privileged confidents such as: Lord Hervey, Vice Chamberlain to Queen Caroline of Anspach; consort of George II; Richard Rush; American Ambassador to the Court of St James's under the Prince Regent; and Marie Mallet, maid of honour to Queen Victoria. They were all privy to gossip as they roamed the drawing rooms and backstairs of royal palaces.

The royal participants sometimes recorded their hopes and expectations in journals and letters to

freely and reputedly 'ran out in the conduits'. At the west door of St Paul's, the church which was destroyed by the Great Fire of 1666 and from whose ashes the present cathedral rose, there was a wooden gangway which had been set up for the wedding. This led inside to the entrance to the choir. At the end was a raised platform or stage, draped in scarlet, where the bride and groom would stand. On one side sat the King and Queen and on the other, representatives of the Corporation of London. Both Arthur and Catherine wore white satin. They were married by the Archbishop of Canterbury and mass was celebrated following the ceremony. Catherine was led from the church not by her husband, but by his ten-year-old brother, the Duke of York.

Henry, Duke of York, was to become heir to the throne less than six months after the wedding on the death of Prince Arthur. In 1509 he too married Catherine of Aragon and in the same year succeeded his father as King.

Henry VIII was a monarch who revelled in display; among his six marriages were some examples of great pomp and ceremony. Discretion, however, dictated that others were more modest affairs. For

OPPOSITE PAGE: *This painting is said, by some authorities, to depict the wedding of Henry VII and Elizabeth of York, in 1486. The Queen's gown cost £11 5s 6d. Artist unknown. (The Lady Braye, Courtauld)*

THIS PAGE, FAR LEFT: *Henry VIII. Although a much married monarch, his weddings varied greatly in the degree of display that surrounded them, and in the preparations made for them. By J. V. Cleve. (National Portrait Gallery).* LEFT: *Anne of Cleves by Holbein. It was this portrait which convinced Henry VIII of her beauty and led him to marry her. (The Louvre)*

example, he hardly waited for the axe to fall upon Ann Boleyn's neck before he tied the matrimonial knot with Catherine Howard and set about his obsession of fathering a son.

The interrelated theme of power politics and regal cunning may be seen again in the marital history of Princess Mary, issue of the marriage between Henry VIII and Catherine of Aragon. She was first betrothed and married by proxy at the age of two and a half to the Dauphin, eldest son of the French King. At this tender age her part in the marriage service was necessarily passive. Cardinal Wolsey, however, placed on her finger a diamond ring, and the French Admiral Bonnivet, who acted as proxy for the Dauphin, symbolically sealed the union by passing it over the second joint. For her first essay into matrimony Mary wore a dress of cloth of gold and a black velvet cap decorated with jewels. She was carried in the arms of her nurse and acquitted herself well, not crying once during the service or even during the Bishop of Durham's long sermon extolling the virtues of marriage. In fact the marriage was never consummated. The shifting sands of diplomacy rendered it inappropriate to Henry's plans. There were other abortive betrothals before Mary came to the throne in 1553.

Although not an attractive woman by contemporary standards, Mary, as Queen of England, was a beguiling prospect for the Spanish, and Philip of Spain, son of Charles V, was to marry Mary in 1554.

In June 1554 Philip left Spain for England. His bodyguard were dressed in liveries of red and

yellow with silk facings. Since his father had not concerned himself to limit Philip's wardrobe, the twenty-six-year-old Prince had spent hugely at his tailors. There were suits of crimson velvet, grey satin and white silk decorated with a profusion of jewels packed into his cabin. One jacket in particular was described as covered in gold chain and silver braid while some of his clothes were so encrusted with precious stones that it was not possible to see the cloth beneath. Philip was also fond of jewellery, including gold chains worn around the shoulders. All of these props were eminently suitable to a king and, in fact, even during the voyage Philip began signing letters Phillipus Rex, in anticipation of his future status.

He arrived in Southampton in July of 1554, remaining there for a few days before making his way to Winchester, where he was to meet Mary for their marriage. The poor weather on the journey to Winchester forced Philip to stop at a hospital outside the city to change his sodden white doublet and hose – wet through despite the red felt cloak he wore – to black and white velvet decorated with gold. His retinue were not so fortunate and they had to follow tired and drenched in their liveries. In fact, Philip decided that he must change once more for his first encounter with his future wife. This time he chose a doublet and trunk hose of white kid worn with a surcoat decorated with gold and silver thread. The frequent changes of costume were effective. He was described as 'perfect and manly'.

Mary, some years older than Philip did not impress the Spanish. Short, thin and myopic, she was dressed in a plain gown of black velvet. One of Philip's retinue recorded that he felt she was not at all beautiful, while Ruy Gomez remarked, perhaps more diplomatically, that she was 'rather older than we had been told'.

The wedding took place on 25 July, the feast of St James, in Winchester Cathedral. The church was hung with tapestries for the occasion and a stage had been set up for the spectacle. Philip wore a white doublet and breeches, together with a mantle which Mary had presented to him the previous day. Of cloth of gold, it was trimmed and lined with crimson velvet, and decorated with gold thistles and pearl buttons. With this he wore the Collar of the

Order of the Garter, another present from Mary.

Mary was attired in a gown of rich brocade with a long train. The sleeves were encrusted with pearls, gold and diamonds. There is, in a detailed inventory, a description of what may well be Mary's wedding dress:

A French gowne of riche golde tissue with a border of purple Satten allover embroidered with perles of damaske golde and pearle lyned with purple Taphata . . one round kirtle of golde tissue with a brode border embroidered with damaske silver and some pearle the hinder part white Satten lyned with white Taphata.

With such splendour, a contrast from the plain dress she wore to her first meeting with Philip, it was said she outshone everyone and that the jewels on her gown blinded those present. She was attended by fifty ladies, all in cloth of gold and silver, who were described by contemporaries as having the appearance of angels. After the service a herald explained the significance of the union in terms of the power that now accrued to the couple. They were, he declared:

Philip and Mary, and by the Grace of God, King and Queen of England, France, Naples, Jerusalem and Ireland, defenders of the faith, Princes of Spain and Sicily, Archdukes of Austria, Dukes of Milan, Burgundy and Brabant, Counts of Hapsburg, Flanders and Tyrol.

At the banquet which followed the wedding ceremony, held in the bishop's palace, only Mary and Philip were seated – everyone else was obliged

OPPOSITE PAGE, LEFT: Princess Elizabeth, daughter of Charles I, who married Frederick, Elector of the German Palatinate. Their grandson inherited the British throne in 1714. (National Portrait Gallery). RIGHT: Mary I and Philip of Spain. The dogs may have been intended as a symbol of fidelity. Oil painting attributed to Ewath. (Woburn Abbey)

THIS PAGE, ABOVE: A commemorative coin of Philip of Spain, who made the journey to England to marry Queen Mary, eldest daughter of Henry VIII.

to stand. Subtle distinctions indicated that Mary was not to be seen as subservient to her husband. For example, the chair she sat upon was more finely made than Philip's and while she ate from a gold plate, he dined from silver. With the exception of Don Inigo de Mendoza, only English nobles were permitted the honour of serving the couple, thereby firmly putting the Spanish in their place. When dancing later in the day, Mary proved to be a more accomplished performer than her husband, and any Englishman present the equal or superior of his Spanish counterpart.

The guests departed by nine o'clock when Mary and Philip were taken to separate apartments to dine, before preparing for the wedding night. The bed was blessed by the Chancellor, but, as the Spanish Calendar remarked, 'What happened that night only they knew'.

Since there was no issue from this marriage, and Queen Elizabeth never married, the succession passed to James VI of the House of Stuart, who ruled over the United Kingdom as James I. He had married Anne of Denmark in Oslo in 1589. Of their seven children the first to marry was Elizabeth. Her husband was to be Frederick V Elector Palatine. This marriage is historically important: from it descended the House of Hanover which would rule Britain from 1714.

The bride's mother, Anne, was not entirely happy with the marriage because she felt her future son-in-law's royal status beneath her daughter's. Frederick, however, was a popular choice and the marriage seems to have been a genuine love match. It was celebrated on St Valentine's Day, 1613, in the Banqueting House, Whitehall. Frederick, wearing a suit of cloth of silver was attended by sixteen nobles, all bachelors; the number a reference to his age. His bride also wore silver, with white, and a gold crown set with pearls; her hair was worn long, as a sign of maidenhood. She was attended by sixteen bridesmaids. The splendour of the bride and groom was eclipsed by the King who reputedly wore jewels that day worth £600,000.

The celebrations of the marriage had begun the day before with a mock battle on the Thames, in which the British forces were victorious over the 'Turks', whose castle, specially built for the occasion near the Palace of the Archbishop of Canterbury, was satisfactorily sacked. A grand display of fireworks modelled on that which had celebrated Prince Henry's investiture as Prince of Wales only two years previously, followed.

After the wedding, masques were performed together with a special version of *The Tempest*, for which Shakespeare had specially written additional material.

Elizabeth's brother, Charles, succeeded his father in 1625 and in the same year married Henrietta

BELOW: *The landing of Catherine of Braganza at Portsmouth, shortly before her marriage to Charles II. (National Portrait Gallery)*

Maria of France. The marriage and the reign were cruelly cut short in 1649 when Charles I was executed. His conflict with Parliament had led to the Civil War and, after his death, to the period of the Commonwealth when Britain was ruled as a republic. The monarchy was restored in 1660 with the accession of Charles II who, two years later, married Catherine of Braganza, Infanta of Spain.

Charles II was known as something of a connoisseur of female beauty. He had been married, according to custom, by proxy, before he had seen his wife. After a long and eventful journey Catherine arrived at Portsmouth, where the King's practised eye could assess his wife in the flesh. First impressions were not promising. He is said to have exclaimed afterwards to one of his advisors, Colonel Legge, that he had been brought not a woman but a bat! Catherine was short, swarthy, with protruding teeth. In due course, however, Charles could write to his sister in France that 'I must tell you I think

myself very happy, I was married the day before yesterday . . .'.

There were two services. In private there was a Roman Catholic ceremony which was surrounded by the greatest secrecy because it was feared the Court and public would be alarmed if it were learned that their King had been married according to the Catholic rite. There were both liturgical objections and deep-seated fears for the political independence of the country from both Rome and Catholic France. As we shall see, this theme was to emerge time and again in royal marriages.

The secret ceremony was followed by the public Protestant service on the afternoon of 21 May. Catherine was wearing a dress of rose pink, decorated with knots of blue ribbon. Afterwards these knots were, one by one, detached from her gown by Lady Suffolk, Lady of the Bedchamber, and distributed as favours to the royal family and the

ABOVE: *Charles II and Catherine of Braganza. Charles wears the mantle of the Order of the Garter. (Duke of Northumberland).* BELOW: *Charles I and his consort Henrietta Maria commemorative medal. Charles has the badge of the Order of the Garter around his neck.*

Court. The first love knot was given to the King's brother, James, Duke of York.

James, much to his brother's disapproval, had married Anne Hyde in 1660. She was maid of honour to the Duke's sister and, as such, not regarded by the rest of the family as a suitable match. The young Duke of Gloucester remarked that she 'smelt of the green bag', a reference to her father's work as a lawyer. The marriage lasted seven years until the Duchess's death. She bore James two daughters, Mary and Anne.

James was urged to remarry after her death, not least by his brother the King, who by then realized that he was unlikely to father any legitimate heirs himself. Lord Peterborough, an ageing advisor, was despatched on a European tour to inspect what was currently available. His choice fell on an Italian, Mary Beatrice, the daughter of the Duke of Modena. At fifteen she was nearly a quarter of a century younger than James and wanted to become a nun. It was not to be her calling, although she protested that James was more suited in age to her aunt. She found herself married by proxy on 30 September 1673, with Lord Peterborough standing in place of James.

The second marriage took place at Dover shortly after Mary Beatrice landed from the Continent on 21 November. James was pleased with his wife, who is described as being tall and slim, her pale complexion set off by her black hair and large dark eyes.

After he had become King on the death of

Charles II, James fathered a son and it was this child, together with James's increasing leaning towards the Roman Catholic religion, that set in train the events which were to topple James from the throne. Indeed the child is said to have been the inspiration for the traditional nursery rhyme 'Hush a Bye Baby', which contains the line 'When the bough breaks, the cradle will fall'. Although James's monarchy was blown away, the Stuart dynasty did not fall entirely. The throne went to Mary, James's eldest daughter by his marriage to Anne Hyde.

LEFT: *Princess Mary, afterwards Queen. A statuesque beauty, she wept when told she was to be married to William of Orange. Portrait by Peter Lely. (Reproduced by gracious permission of Her Majesty The Queen).*
ABOVE: *The Duke of York, afterwards James II, with his first wife, Anne Hyde. (National Portrait Gallery)*

TOP RIGHT: *Princess Anne, younger daughter of the Duke of York, and her husband, Prince George of Denmark. The medal commemorates their marriage on St Anne's Day, 28 July 1683.*

Princess Mary had married William of Orange in 1677. Although the marriage was a success in emotional terms – after her death William was devastated and he wore a locket with a lock of her hair in it to his dying day – neither its inception nor its celebration boded well. Mary, almost the last person at court to be told of her fate, burst into tears at the news of her impending marriage. At the ceremony she again wept and William was described as looking unhappy. Perhaps Mary's disquiet was based on the clear differences in temperament and outlook. She was gregarious; he was stiff and formal. Moreover, where as she was a statuesque beauty of five foot eleven inches, he was almost six inches shorter. The actual marriage ceremony was held in Mary's bedroom in St James's Palace at nine o'clock, in the evening of Sunday 4 November. It was a quiet affair, the solemnity of the occasion lightened by the vulgar remarks of King Charles II, whose parting comment, as he drew the curtains on the marriage bed was, 'So nephew, to your work! Hey St George for England'.

This invocation of the patron saint of the country not withstanding, the union bore no fruit; the throne passed on William's death to his sister-in-law Anne.

Anne had been married in 1683 to Prince George of Denmark. He was described by an anonymous observer as he rode down Whitehall as 'a very comely person, fair hair, a few pock marks in his visage, but of a very decent and graceful behaviour'. Not one of nature's greatest wits, many found him a dull fellow indeed. Charles II complained that: 'I have tried him drunk and I have tried him sober, and drunk or sober there is nothing to him'. Nevertheless he was married to Princess Anne on 28 July in the Chapel Royal at St James's.

Despite many pregnancies Anne failed to produce an heir to the throne who survived her. Therefore, when she died in 1714 the British crown went under the terms of the Act of Succession – which was designed to secure the Protestant line – to the Elector of Hanover, who came to England as George I. And it is with the wedding of George I that our story begins.

RICH BROCADES AND
FINE JEWELS

IN the eighteenth century, royal marriages continued to centre around political gain, extending influence and cementing alliances. Throughout this period in Britain the monarch and the Court remained the focus of political activity and so royal marriages were essentially court events: the public appreciation of the wedding was incidental. This necessarily had important influence on the dress worn at royal weddings. Ladies and gentlemen wore court dress, which implied specific styles and the ostentatious display of wealth.

On all important occasions female members of the royal family wore a dress known as the *corps de robe*, or royal robe. Mrs Delany, whose letters recording her observations of the Court at this time are an invaluable source for the social historian and historian of dress, describes such a dress in her account of the wedding of the Princess Royal in 1734:

> The Princess of Orange's dress was the prettiest thing that ever was seen – a *corps de robe* that is in plain English, a stiff-bodied gown. The eight peers' daughters that held up the train were in the same sort of dress – all white and silver with great quantities of jewels in their hair.

Observing the procession which took place during the Coronation of King George in 1727, she noted additional splendid examples:

> Lady Fanny Nassau [who was one of the ladies that bore up the train of the Queen] looked exceedingly well; her clothes were fine and a very becoming pink coloured satin, the gown (which was stiff-bodied) embroidered with silver, the petticoat covered with a trimming answerable. Princess Anne . . . and her sisters held up the tip of the train; they were dressed in stiff-bodied gowns of silver tissue; embroidered or quite covered with silver trimming, with diadems on their head and purple mantles edged with ermine and vast long trains.

Descriptions such as these, together with observations of the ceremonial and the principal characters concerned, provide us with a vivid picture of Hanoverian weddings.

The court suits of the gentlemen were as splendid as those of the ladies. Vast fortunes were spent on suits of silk and velvet decorated with paste and jewels. For most of the century, royal bridegrooms wore court suits to their weddings, usually with the Star of an Order of Knighthood on the breast. This both proclaimed status and added more splendour to their garb. Although the gaining of political advantage and the security of the dynasty was always uppermost in the minds of those charged with arranging these marriages, the personal preferences of the Royal Family began to play a role.

Although Queen Caroline, consort to George II, insisted to her Vice Chamberlain, Lord Hervey, that she sought neither to encourage nor to discourage her eldest daughter's marriage to the Prince of Orange, one wonders how free a choice she had. She was, said the Queen 'absolutely at liberty to accept or reject it'.

PHYSICAL attraction to the proposed spouse was felt to be a positive advantage when marriages were arranged. George I, at the time the eldest son of the Elector of Hanover, found his sixteen-year-old bride Sophia Dorothea a very beguiling proposition. She had inspired in George a passion of which his mother felt him incapable.

OPPOSITE PAGE: *George III, grandson of George II. Portrait in his coronation robes by A. Ramsay, dated 1761. His wedding took place shortly before the Coronation. (Reproduced by gracious permission of Her Majesty The Queen)*

ABOVE: *Sophia Charlotte von Kielmansegg, George I's half-sister and rumoured mistress. Also known as 'the Elephant'. (Weidenfeld)*

Despite the attraction to one another, this marriage, which was to found the Hanoverian dynasty that ruled Britain from 1714, was designed primarily to extend the influence of the house of Hanover and produce offspring. Essentially it was an arranged marriage.

What was not arranged, or foreseen, was the passionate attachment Sophia developed for the dashing Swedish Count Konigsmark. George was frequently away from Hanover; for example, in 1684, he was busily engaged in fighting the Turkish army – and he had, by 1691, taken Melusine van der Schulenberg as his mistress. Sophia responded with her affair with Konigsmark, which involved the exchange of a series of passionate love letters. These, together with the gossip that surrounded the lovers and rumours of an elopement, led to the Count's death in 1694. He was on his way to Sophia's apartment in Hanover when he was probably assassinated by courtiers loyal to George. His body was thrown into a nearby river.

Sophia was confined to a castle in Ahlen in Germany and the marriage was dissolved soon after.

So it was that George I took up residence at Kensington Palace in London with his mistress von der Schulenberg and his half-sister, Charlotte von

Kielmansegg, two ladies whose respective physiques soon led them to being known as 'the Beanpole' and 'the Elephant'.

George was succeeded by his son, George II, in 1727. It is with the marriages of his children that we uncover a rich seam of evidence concerning the conduct and ceremonial of the English court, including the royal marriages.

The eldest daughter of George II, Anne, Princess Royal, was the first to marry. Her chosen partner was the Prince of Orange. Despite her mother's apparent indifference to the match there were compelling reasons for the attachment: the Hanoverian house would form a connection with the House of Orange, a powerful Protestant family. The Prince was, however, neither universally admired nor respected. Lord Hervey was hypercritical in his memoirs, describing Prince William as 'a miserable match both in point of man and fortune, his figure is deformed and his estate not clear £12,000 a year'. On the other hand, Lord Chesterfield described the prospective groom as having 'extreme good parts'. His face was 'handsome' and although his shape was 'not so advantageous as could be wished . . . not near so bad as I had heard represented'.

Most important was the magic name of Orange, which even Hervey felt tipped the balance in the Prince's favour. The Princess really had no choice, whatever her mother might say – it was her diplomatic responsibility to make the match. According to Hervey, either she was to marry 'this piece of deformity from Holland' or die 'an ancient maid in her Royal convent of St James's'. The Princess was attractive, with a fine complexion, albeit marked, which was not unusual at the time, by smallpox.

The date for the alliance of these two young persons – and the two houses of Hanover and Orange – was fixed for November 1733, but when the Prince fell ill, it was postponed until 14 March of the following year. The ceremony was performed in the Chapel Royal at St James's Palace, which was fitted up especially for the wedding. A covered way was built from the King's apartments in the palace, through the adjoining garden to the chapel. In the gallery there was ample room for four thousand guests, who would be shepherded by the King's Bodyguard of the Yeomen of the Guard, wearing

TOP LEFT: Melusine von der Schulenberg, mistress of George I, by whom he had three daughters. Her slender figure gave her the nickname of 'Beanpole'. (Weidenfeld). OPPOSITE PAGE: The marriage of the Princess Royal, eldest daughter of George II, to Prince William of Orange. The Chapel Royal at St James's Palace was decorated for the event. (National Portrait Gallery)

distinctive ceremonial uniforms. Essentially, the costumes of these guards survive in style to this day.

In overall charge of the ceremonial was Lord Hervey and he later recorded that almost everyone was happy with the arrangements he made, with the exception of the Irish peers. A disagreement sparked between the Irish and the English barons as to whom should have precedence in the procession. Hervey decided the English barons should lead; the Irish viscounts and earls petitioned the King and then the Cabinet upon this point of honour and the quarrel spluttered on until a few days before the wedding when the Irish eventually declared in disgust that they would not attend.

As with all of the weddings examined in this period, the ceremony took place in the evening and those taking part in the procession were required to assemble at seven o'clock. There were, in fact, two main processions, that of the groom and that of the bride; the former always entering first. Preceding the Prince of Orange into the chapel was a band of fifes, drums and trumpets, with the sergeant trumpeter leading.

He wore his ceremonial collar of gold interlinked S's, and bore a large mace as a symbol of office. The band filed off to either side of the door. They were followed by the Master of Ceremonies, an important royal household officer who took charge of the event. Next came the Gentleman Usher to the groom, flanked by two officers from the College of Heralds. Finally the Prince and his retinue followed. The groom wore a gold and silver court suit and the Collar of the Order of the Garter. Even Lord Hervey remarked that there was 'nothing very strikingly disagreeable about him'.

The Prince was brought by his supporters to a velvet-covered stool which had been placed before the King's throne. Around him, the chapel had been lavishly decorated. Velvet, gold and silver tissue, fringes, tassels and sconces all contributed to a dazzling effect. The King had spent a great deal of money on the proceedings, although Hervey could not restrain himself from remarking afterwards that he might have more wisely given the money to the bride.

The Lord Chamberlain collected the Princess. Like the groom she was accompanied by a Gentle-

man Usher, and walked between two Officers of Arms. As described by Mrs Delany, the bride wore a silver tissue *corps de robe*, her coronet as a royal princess, and a mantle or train of velvet and ermine, which was supported by no less than ten ladies, all of them daughters of dukes or earls, with those of higher social precedence being chosen to walk nearest to the Princess herself. All of the female attendants wore white gowns.

The Princess was conducted to a stool next to the Prince of Orange and they were seated to wait while the King and Queen, accompanied by the great officers of the household and peers, were ushered in. Not until all of these persons were seated could the service, conducted by the Bishop of London, begin. Afterwards the processions wound their way back into the palace.

Although the liturgical part of the marriage was over, there was additional and important court ceremonial to be observed. Even at this date there remained, in the public life of the monarch, vestiges of the mediaeval concept of Kingship, when the sovereign had displayed himself to his court, while eating, for example. At about eleven o'clock, the newly married couple and the entire royal family dined before the Court who were admitted to the state ballroom of St James's.

Two hours later the bride and groom retired. They were to be viewed in their bedchamber by the nobility in what was described as their 'rich undresses'. It was at this point that Hervey found the appearance of the Prince 'indescribable'. He wore a rich brocade gown which, combined with his build,

ABOVE: *Sophia Dorothea, wife of George I. Detail from a painting by Jacques Vaillon. (Weidenfeld).* OPPOSITE PAGE: *The Princess Royal, eldest daughter of George II. A marriage portrait by J. Amigoni. She wore her mantle of velvet and ermine, and her coronet for the wedding. (Reproduced by gracious permission of Her Majesty The Queen)*

had the unfortunate effect of making him appear 'headless' and 'without legs'. The Queen was horrified at her daughter's fate. Although gallantly – and perhaps uncharacteristically – Hervey reassured her that in time the Princess would not notice her husband's shortcomings, the Queen described her son-in-law as 'a monster'.

The marriage was, however, a success in domestic political terms. The name of the House of Orange worked its magic. The county of Kent, for example, sent a loyal address to the King, in which the memory of that earlier William of Orange, who had led the 'happy revolution of immortal memory', was invoked. The address congratulated the King for making an auspicious alliance, one which promised a glorious future: 'What may we not then expect when both Houses are so happily united'.

It was, in fact, the prospect of increased trade which in many eyes outweighed all else. As a measure of this, when he made his first public appearance after the marriage, the Prince was taken by the King and the Prince of Wales to the House of Lords to be naturalized. Before this ceremony was observed, the King demonstrated his attitude to the marriage by first consenting to the Salt Bill and to duties on beer sold in Scotland.

Although there were inevitably individual eccentricities in the marriage of the Prince and Princess of Orange, it set a pattern which was repeated again and again in royal weddings during that century, and up until 1818. The timing of the ceremony, the location of St James's Palace and the stately and magnificent procession were all to be repeated in the weddings of George II's children and his grandchildren as well.

THE wedding of the Prince of Wales, Frederick Louis, was of greater dynastic importance since he was heir to the throne. By 1735, at age twenty-nine, he had, as was quite common, a number of mistresses. He had recently put aside a Miss Vane and was tiring of Lady Archibald Hamilton, whose beauty was in any case fading.

His father, in Germany for his summer visit to the Hanoverian estates was introduced to Princess Augusta of Saxe-Coburg and he decided on the spot that she was a suitable bride for his eldest son.

He immediately wrote to tell the Queen that she should inform Frederick of his impending marriage. Although father and son often quarrelled, on the matter of his marriage the Prince was compliant. When told that the King would demand the hand of Princess Augusta if he wished it, he replied, 'whoever his Majesty thought a proper match would be agreeable to him'. Lord Delaware, the King's treasurer, was commissioned to travel to Germany and negotiate the marriage. Hervey said that there was no better man for the job – his Lordship was so 'long, lank and awkward' that he would not excite passion in the bride and therefore not incur the jealousy of the groom.

The marriage treaty was hurriedly drawn up and the Princess despatched from her home to England. On 17 April she was met at the Hague by the Prince and Princess of Orange, and sailed two days later for England on the yacht *William and Mary*. Although a strong gale blew during the voyage the Princess landed safely at Greenwich and from there was taken in one of the King's coaches to London itself.

In the capital, preparations had been made for the wedding. The Chapel Royal at St James's had been extensively refurbished for the occasion. Orders had been given for the workmen to set up lanterns, reguild chairs and provide gold tabby to make festoons and roses to decorate the room. Hangings

ABOVE: *Princess Augusta,
portrait by C. Philips, dated
1736. She was described by
a contemporary as being 'of
strong mind'. (Reproduced
by gracious permission of
Her Majesty The Queen)*

The Princess made her way to Lambeth and from there to Whitehall in the royal barge, completing the journey to St James's in a sedan chair, to meet and marry a Prince she had never seen. She was seventeen years old and spoke no English. Hervey described her as tall and rather awkward, 'a good deal awry, her arms long', but wearing fine clothes and jewels. Horace Walpole, who later came to dislike her, felt that she 'was of strong mind' and a good match for the Prince.

On her wedding day it was, however, not her mind but the visual impact she would make that was of paramount importance. She wore on her head her crown as Princess of Wales, which was set with diamonds. Her dress of silver was decorated with diamonds, and her robes of state, which were described by the *Gentleman's Magazine*, were of crimson velvet decorated with rows of ermine. They were carried by four attendants, all daughters of dukes or earls and all wearing versions of the bride's dress, valued at the time at £20,000 each.

The groom, the King, Queen and the Court, entered the chapel in their respective processions. The service over, supper was finished by ten-thirty whereupon the couple were conducted separately to prepare for the wedding night.

On this occasion the King paid his eldest son the compliment of helping him into his nightshirt and cap. According to Hervey, the headgear was several inches higher than the tall mitre caps of the King's Grenadiers and definitely did not enhance the appearance of the groom.

Meanwhile, Princess Augusta was helped into her nightclothes by her new sister-in-law and she was put to bed. The King and the Prince were then admitted — and after them, the whole court — to view the couple sitting up in bed. They could admire the Prince's gold brocade nightdress and his tall cap of fine lace.

Those attending the wedding wore fine court dress. The King's suit was of gold brocade, decorated with large silver flowers, with diamond buttons and the Star of the Garter, set with diamonds, on the left breast. The Queen wore a yellow silk dress decorated with pearls and diamonds. The courtiers, including the dukes of Grafton, Newcastle and St Albans, the Earl of Albemarle, and

of crimson velvet with gold fringes decorated the walls and the floor under the throne was covered with gold and silver tabby. The music gallery was hung with baize; even the canopy and the three crowns over the throne were repaired and restored to their former glory.

Cy commence le liure dit grace entiere sur le
fait du gouuinemet dun pri
N lan de septante trente. xe.
enant quatorze ceus de sente
ung prince de royal noblesse
Qui en age de icunesse.
st grant et excellent seigneur.
Qedonne a estre greigneur.
Car succession naturelle

Abriß Deß Triumphfewerwercks, Bei. Churfurstlich: Pfaltz Heimfuhrung, Gehalten

9 Junij 1613 Jnuent. W. Harnister

PREVIOUS PAGE: *Prince Arthur reading from the roll, and hearing mass. By Bernard Andre. (British Library)*

LEFT: *Firework display to celebrate the wedding of Princess Elizabeth and Frederick Elector of the German Palatinate, 1612.*
ABOVE: *Front and back of the commemorative medal manufactured to mark the wedding of Henry VII and Elizabeth of York.*

OVERLEAF: *Sophia Dorothea, wife of George, Elector of Hanover, later George I, with her children. Painting by Jacques Vaillon. (Weidenfeld)*

PREVIOUS PAGE: *Charles I wearing robes of State and the collar of the Order of the Garter. Oil painting by Van Dyck. (Reproduced by gracious permission of Her Majesty The Queen)*

LEFT: *The marriage of George, Prince of Wales, and Caroline of Brunswick in St James's Palace, 1795. Oil painting by Henry Singleton. (Reproduced by gracious permission of Her Majesty The Queen)*

OVERLEAF: *Marriage of Princess Charlotte and Prince Leopold in Carlton House, 1816. Oil sketch by R. Westall. (Reproduced by gracious permission of Her Majesty The Queen)*

PREVIOUS PAGE: *Oil painting of the wedding of Queen Victoria and Prince Albert of Saxe-Coburg, in the Chapel Royal at St James's Palace. (Robert Opie Collection)*

ABOVE: *Wedding of Princess Louise and the Marquess of Lorne in St George's Chapel, Windsor, 1871. Painting by Sydney Hall. (Reproduced by gracious permission of Her Majesty The Queen).*

RIGHT: *Sketch of the wedding dress of Grand Duchess Marie of Russia, who was married to Prince Albert in 1874. (Reproduced by gracious permission of Her Majesty The Queen)*

RIGHT: *Watercolour by Queen Victoria of the dress worn by her bridesmaids in 1840. (Reproduced by gracious permission of Her Majesty The Queen).*
BELOW: *Coloured engraving of the bridesmaids selected for Princess Alexandra of Denmark in 1863. Each bridesmaid was the eldest daughter of a peer. Coloured engraving by R. Dudley. (Private Collection)*

Prince Albert Edward and Princess Alexandra of Denmark at their wedding in 1863. Oil painting by W. P. Frith. (Reproduced by gracious permission of Her Majesty The Queen)

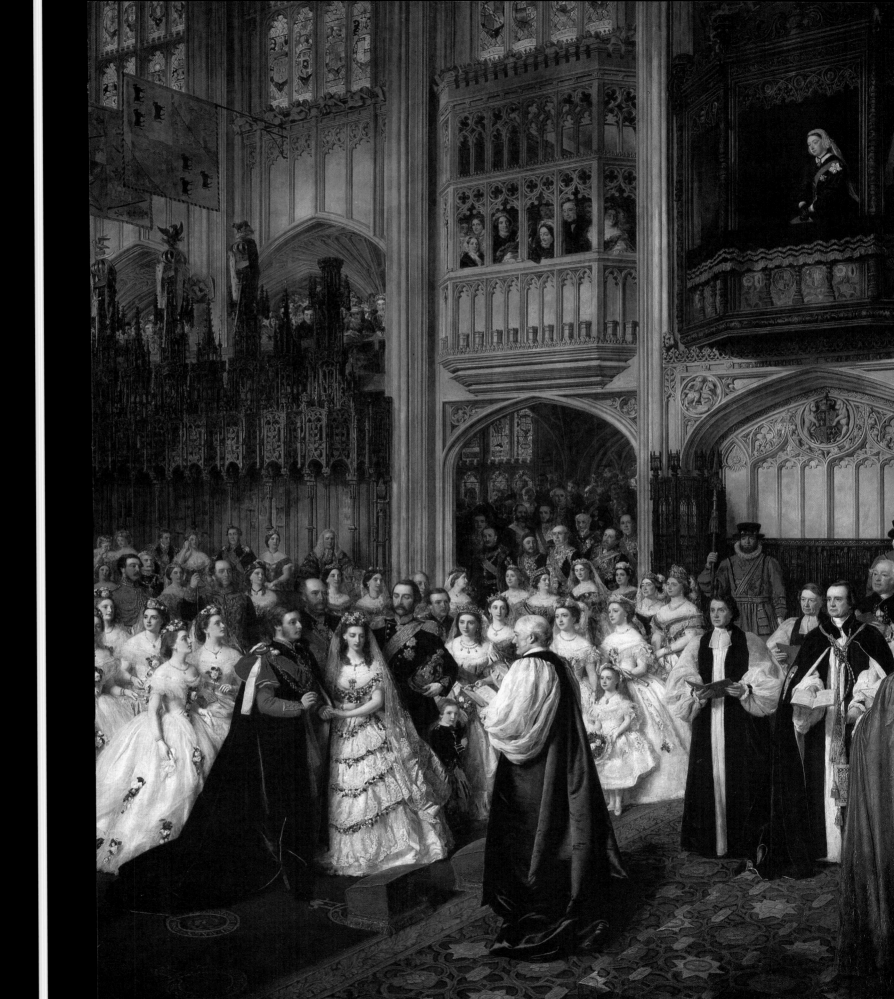

Lord Hervey, all wore gold brocade, each suit costing between £300 and £500.

The Duke of Marlborough distinguished himself by wearing white velvet while others wore gold brocade waistcoats embroidered with large flowers. According to the patriotic *Gentleman's Magazine*, all of the better-looking suits were of English manufacture, 'the few which were French did not come up to these in richness, goodness or fancy'. The ladies were described in their court dresses of gold or silver brocade, with lower sleeves than were usually seen at court.

Hervey says there were various reports of 'what did and did not pass this night. The Queen and Lord Hervey agreed that the bride looked so extremely refreshed the next morning, that they concluded she had slept very sound'.

The activities of the wedding night were in a sense irrelevant once the couple had been viewed in bed by the Court – clearly an heir would in time be produced. In the meantime, the magnificence of the clothing and the impact of the refurbished chapel would have made their mark on society and the foreign ministers who attended. The Hanoverian monarchy's reputation for splendour and longevity had been reaffirmed.

B Y contrast the marriage of the King's second daughter, Princess Mary, warranted only a passing reference in contemporary journals. Four years after the marriage of his son, George II received a proposal from the Landgrave of Hesse that his son should marry Princess Mary. When he informed Parliament of the prospective alliance, the King pointed out that it would clearly bolster Protestant power in Europe. An expenditure of £40,000 was duly voted for the Princess's dowry. Princess Mary was not to see her future husband until the day of her wedding in Cassel four months later. A ceremony of espousal had been performed in the Chapel Royal on 8 March 1740, when the Duke of Cumberland acted as proxy for Ferdinand of Hesse. It was on 2 July that the Princess was met by her Prince at Amelienthal, where he embraced her, it was reported, 'with very great tenderness' and shortly afterwards married her according to the rite of the Calvinist church.

T HE popular historical image of George III is both sad and inaccurate. He is recalled as the monarch who lost the American Colonies and went mad, talking to trees in Windsor Park under the impression that they were other kings and princes. Yet this is the man who, at the age of eighteen, was

ABOVE: *Frederick, Prince of Wales, wearing Garter robes. Portrait by C. Philips. (Reproduced by gracious permission of Her Majesty The Queen)*

Painted by W. M. Craig. *Engraved by J. Rogers.*

First meeting of George III. with the Princess Charlotte of Mecklenburg Strelitz.

described as being of modest disposition and a healthy vigorous constitution, and whose wedding in 1761 was hailed as the crowning glory to his throne. S. Bowden published the following verse in September 1761:

> 'Britannia's monarch, whom three realms obey
> And the more spacious kingdoms of the sea
> Tho blest with all the splendour of the throne
> Still reigned unhappy while he reigned alone'

His bride was epitomized as:

> 'A beauteous nymph – in whose illustrious line
> Heroes and Kings thro distant ages shine'

A great deal was expected of the marriage of George III with Charlotte of Mecklenburg-Strelitz. The King had been a bachelor for nearly twenty-three years, although he had formed serious liaisons with, amongst others, Lady Sarah Lennox, described by chronicler, Sir Nathanial Wraxall, as 'one of the most beautiful young women of high rank in the kingdom', and a Quaker lady, Hannah Lightfoot, whom, it was said, he at one time intended to marry.

George's father, Frederick Prince of Wales, pre-deceased his own father, so that from the age of thirteen he was heir to the throne occupied by his grandfather George II. George II appears to have attempted to choose his grandson's wife as he had his sons. One of the daughters of the Duchess of Brunswick Wolfenbuttel was discussed as a possible bride but, in the end, nothing came of it.

When George inherited the throne in 1761, he realized that he needed a consort. Colonel David Graham was despatched to view what the German Protestant states had to offer and to report back confidentially to the King. Graham was most impressed by Sophia Charlotte, the youngest daughter of Louis Frederick, Duke of Mecklenburg-Strelitz. Charlotte was then eighteen years old and perfectly unaware of the reason for the British colonel's visit.

She was not tall and contemporaries felt that she was too thin to be termed beautiful, but she had a fine head of dark brown hair which complemented her pale complexion. As Walpole said, she 'looks sensible and genteel, her forehead low, her nose very well, except the nostrils spreading too wide.

Her mouth has the same fault, but her teeth are good'.

Happy with the reports he had of the Princess, George instructed his mother to write and demand Charlotte's hand in marriage. The negotiations were conducted with great secrecy. It was said that few besides Lord Bute and the King knew what was planned. On 3 July 1761, Bute could contain himself no longer and wrote to the Duke of Bedford that 'the King intends to declare his resolution of taking a consort to his bed'. Once the news that the intended candidate was Princess Charlotte leaked out, courtiers and politicians had to consult their maps of Europe and genealogical tables of European aristocracy. Walpole wrote that 'perhaps there are not six men in England who know that such a princess exists'. The King's emmissary to Mecklenburg was to be Lord Harcourt – 'If he can find the place'.

Although the news was becoming known to a wider audience, at least one of the persons most intimately concerned remained ignorant and uninvolved. Charlotte was not informed of the wedding until negotiations were complete.

Charlotte had lived a quiet life in the duchy. In later life she was to recall that one evening her elder brother informed her that there was to be that night a grand dinner for an ambassador from England and that she was to behave in the most adult manner she could contrive. When Charlotte asked her mother if she should wear her own modest jewels, the Duchess instead presented her with a huge pair of garnet earrings and she was led forthwith into the salon to meet the ambassador.

The Princess must have been slightly naïve, for she still had no idea what had been discussed in her absence, nor any idea why she was the centre of attention: in a place of honour next to the ambassador. They conversed about the King, his marriage prospects and Charlotte asked if George would not marry the Princess of Prussia. It was not until after the meal, when the formal act of betrothal took place, that she finally understood the purpose of the visit and her future.

The betrothal was a curious rite of passage that involved the symbolic consummation of the marriage. Charlotte was led into a room by her brother

OPPOSITE PAGE: George III greeting his bride-to-be, Princess Charlotte of Mecklenburg-Strelitz. Courtiers carry white wands as a badge of office. Painted by W. M. Craig. (The Mansell Collection)

who gave her in marriage to the English ambassador, who acted as the King's proxy. She was then laid upon a sofa and the Englishman placed his foot next to her, the act representing his monarch bedding the Princess. The ritual was by no means unique to Mecklenburg or, indeed, Germany. Similar to the public viewing of the newly wed couple in their marriage bed, it was practised in many European courts at the time – a reminder of how tightly bound by tradition and ancient ritual were the royal courts of the Continent.

After he had symbolically stepped into her bed the ambassador presented the bride with a set of diamond jewellery and the assembled company spent the remainder of the evening passing around the jewels for inspection and admiration.

Afterwards, the Princess recalled that she had, from the moment of the betrothal, seen and known nothing and had been quite bewildered. Her confusion was increased by the insistence of the ambassador that they depart as soon as possible for England. On 17 August, the future Queen of Great Britain set out for her new kingdom.

In London there were great preparations underway. The wedding ceremony was to be followed by the double Coronation. There were problems of crowd control, the correct order of procession, the fitting-up of the Chapel Royal to be put in hand and, not least, the transport arrangements for the Princess upon her arrival.

The Lord Chamberlain's Office executed these matters. The Duke of Devonshire, as Lord Chamberlain, drafted memoranda, sketched the plan of procession and sent out dozens of orders from his office. The High Constable of Westminster was directed, on 30 August, to have sufficient men on hand to prevent hackney carriages coming nearer to the Palace of St James than the end of Pall Mall. No coaches were to enter the courtyard by way of the gateway near the Duke of Cumberland's apartments and sedan chairs were to set their passengers down in Green Cloth Court and leave by a carefully controlled route. It is obvious that one-way traffic systems are not a twentieth-century invention.

No doubt assuming that both the High Constable and Field Marshal Lord Ligonier, who had command of the Household Troops, would carry out his instructions, Devonshire turned his attention to the chapel. He wanted a new throne erected, and to ensure that there was sufficient space for all those who would attend. In the Public Record Office there survives his office's calculations that each person would occupy an average of two feet.

Then there was the matter of the bridesmaids. Requests were sent out to the daughters of peers who were considered eligible for the honour. At least two candidates, Lady Caroline Montagu, daughter of the Duke of Manchester, and Lady Louisa Greville, took several weeks to reply. Anxious officials at the Lord Chamberlain's Office were only reassured that all was well when, barely a month before the wedding, replies were received stating that the ladies would 'esteem it a great honour to be asked to be one of the bridesmaids to the Queen'.

The Lord Chamberlain and his officials were faced with the age-old and delicate problem of the order of precedence of the procession. There were those who recollected the difficulties Lord Hervey had had with the Irish peers at the Prince of Orange's wedding. An inquiry was made of the College of Heralds. Martin Leake, Garter King of Arms, consulted his records to discover how to dispose of the unmarried daughters of peers, the sons of peers and the Irish viscounts and heralds. In a bid to be more fully involved in all of the arrangements, he concluded by pointing out that heralds usually officiated at the weddings and that he would be glad to receive the Lord Chamberlain's commands in relation to the King's forthcoming nuptials.

Not least in his mind was the Lord Chamberlain's responsibility to bring the bride by water from Greenwich to St James's. Robert Wilmot wrote on behalf of the Lord Chamberlain to Colonel Pelham at Greenwich on 29 August 1761 asking if there were tea, coffee 'and all such refreshments proper and that may be wanting' for the Princess's arrival. The military had already conquered this problem and Pelham was able to reply, proudly and by return, that Mr Robinson the confectioner had been at Greenwich some days before and had left 'two servants with coffee, tea, chocolate and everything else relating to a collation'.

OPPOSITE PAGE: *Lady Elizabeth Keppel, wearing the silver and white dress made for her as bridesmaid to Princess Charlotte of Mecklenburg-Strelitz. (Woburn Abbey)*

Everything seemed in order, although only the day before the date set for the ceremony, the College of Arms was still writing to the Lord Chamberlain's Office: 'having heard the Tower guns announce the arrival of the Princess of Mecklenburg' and enquiring if the Lord Chamberlain had approved the ceremonials suggested by the heralds.

As is often the case with English ceremonials, the weather had taken a hand in the affair some days before. On 7 November, the day when the Princess was expected to arrive at Greenwich, crowds turned out to greet their future Queen. They were disappointed. While the royal household had been frantically preparing for the wedding, the royal yacht, with its distinguished cargo, had been buffeted for ten days by gales in the Channel and North Sea. At one time it looked as if Norway and not England would be its ultimate destination. Moreover, the Duchess of Ancaster and the Duchess of Hamilton, who had accompanied the Princess from Germany, were not good sailors. At times during the voyage they must have questioned their bestowed honour of bringing George's chosen Queen to him. Happily, the Princess was only mildly ill for half an hour. While the rest of the party were distinctly unwell, she conversed with the officers on board, played the harpsichord and guitar, and finished her recital with a resounding rendition of 'God Save the King'.

On the 7 September the yacht eventually managed to put into the port of Harwich. While she remained on board, new arrangements were made for the Princess to make her way to London. In due course she was permitted to land and to receive the Mayor and Alderman of the town before continuing to Colchester by coach, where she arrived exhausted to take tea and coffee at five o'clock. Refreshed, she set off once more for Witham where she was to spend the night in the house of Lord Abercorn. She was the object of intense interest everywhere she went and even at dinner that evening the door of the dining room was left open so that, as the *Gentleman's Magazine* pointed out, 'everybody might have the pleasure of seeing Her Highness'.

Early the next day she was off once more. At Mr Dutton's in Romford, the party took coffee. Aware that she was on display, Charlotte had dressed carefully. For the journey she wore a dress of gold brocade, with a stomacher studded with diamonds, her hair dressed with fine lace lappets. She ordered the coach to drive slowly so that she could be seen by as many as possible. According to *Gentleman's Magazine*, there was indeed 'an incredible number of spectators both on horse and on foot'. The coach came through the City, across Islington to Hyde Park, and down Constitution Hill to St James's Palace.

The Princess might be forgiven for supposing that after twenty-three days of travel across Europe and the English Channel, buffeted by gales and enduring the curiosity of her future subjects, she would be permitted a few days' rest – and Charlotte certainly imagined this to be the case. For a moment she did not appreciate the import of a remark made casually by one of her ladies-in-waiting, who looked at her watch and said that they would be late for the wedding and have little time to change.

'Wedding?' exclaimed the Princess, to which came the reply, 'Yes Madam, it is to be at twelve'.

The future Queen of England promptly fainted.

Lavender water was briskly administered to revive her in time for her first encounter with the King. George III stood waiting in the midst of his court at the entrance of St James's Palace. Next to him was the elderly Duke of Grafton and between them, the cushion upon which the Princess was to kneel in obeisance to the King. Initially mistaking Grafton for the King, she was relieved to be corrected; she was then escorted to the palace where she was able to refresh herself and to prepare for her wedding.

The bridal arrangements would not begin until eight o'clock that evening. She entered the chapel preceded by drums and trumpets, with the Vice Chamberlain of the household, her maids of honour and ladies of the bedchamber, and the Lord Chamberlain. From contemporary description she appears to have been wearing a *corps de robe* in white and silver with what Walpole was to describe as her 'endless mantle of violet-coloured velvet, lined with ermine and attempted to be fastened on her shoulder by a bunch of huge pearls'. The weight of the mantle dragged her dress 'half-way down her waist' so that 'the spectators knew as much of her upper half as the King'. The burden was partially relieved by the ten, unmarried daughters of earls and dukes who acted as bride maids – as they were known at the time. They too wore robes of white and silver with diamond coronets on their heads. The Princess's tiara was worth, £60,000 one observer calculated.

The King's procession was even more impressive than that of his bride and he was attired in the Collar of the Order of the Garter.

The Princess was given away by the Duke of Cumberland, the King's younger brother, and the service was conducted by the Archbishop of Canterbury. At the moment that the bride's and groom's hands were joined together, the artillery stationed in Hyde Park fired a salute, which was taken up by the battery at the Tower of London. The Princess was Queen and her long journey over.

Afterwards a 'Nuptial Drawing Room' took place, at which the Court paid its respects to the couple. In London the celebrations went on long into the night, with 'the utmost demonstrations of joy' – as the *Gentleman's Magazine* reported.

The Queen was in no hurry to retire; in fact, it was not until three o'clock in the morning, when the Duke of Cumberland and the Princess Augusta felt unable to stay awake any longer, that Charlotte realized she must prepare for her wedding night. At this time there came a clean break with tradition. The Queen made it clear that only her mother-in-law and two of her own ladies-in-waiting would help her undress and that only her husband, the King, would be admitted to the bedroom. There was to be no ritual court view of the bride and groom in bed together, such as that which took place at the marriage of the Princess Royal and the King's own father. If Charlotte broke tradition she did not, however, end it. Thirty-six years later, on 18 May 1797, her daughter married the Prince of Württemberg and on that night the company once more rose to see a royal couple in bed together.

The celebrations of Charlotte's marriage were far from over; the ensuing days were filled with high-spirited events. There were levées to attend at which 'gentlemen of the first distinction' with the foreign ministers 'all in their grand dresses' paid their compliments. There were court balls, an address to be

Medal commemorating the Coronation of George III and Queen Charlotte. A contemporary wrote: 'They will be a happy couple'.

received from the Mayor and citizens of London, and a family outing to the Drury Lane Playhouse to see a production of *The Rehearsal*. There was a carefully ordered procession to the theatre at which the crowds were so great that the new Queen herself showed signs of fear. The ladies attending her wore the dresses and jewellery they had sported at the wedding; it was a glittering occasion, indeed.

The long voyage and the wedding celebrations took their toll on the young princess from the obscure German duchy. But with the merry-making concluded, and now consort to King George III, she settled down to a reign of more than sixty years. The next year, in 1762, she gave birth to a son, George Augustus, later the Prince of Wales and popularly known as 'Prinny' and the 'First Gentleman of Europe'.

In the meantime she could bask in the glory of her new role and her undoubted popularity; perhaps reading Bowden's verse, published at Frome, on 7 September 1761, with some satisfaction:

Welcome fair nymph! To Albion's happy shore
Whose chalky cliffs look fairer than before
Long may you reign serene to bless this isle
And beauteous offsprings in your image smile
Illustrious infants round the palace play
Born to suppress all arbitrary sway;
Learning and peace, and virtues cause advance
And crush the projects of ambitious France

In these few lines are contained all the elements of an eighteenth-century royal marriage: beauty, children and power politics.

RICHNESS AND FANCY

Born in 1762, George, Prince of Wales, was an extraordinary man with unusual gifts of taste and charm. Although exceptional in many ways, however, his reaction to the first sight of his prospective wife shortly before he was to marry her was neither in the best taste nor especially charming. Hardly able to believe his eyes he turned to an aide, invoked the Almighty, and demanded brandy.

The Prince had been led to this unhappy encounter mainly through his own improvidence and impetuousness. Chronically unable to manage his finances, but greatly skilled in spending money, he increased his personal debts with his years. In 1786 his debts were calculated at over a quarter of a million pounds and, six years later, a little short of half a million. He desperately needed to wipe out these debts and to increase his income; and for this he required the cooperation of his father, with whom he enjoyed relations that were less than cordial. Only one move would bring increased funds and parental approval and that was marriage. He was, in fact, already married to a Mrs Fitzherbert; however, under the terms of the Royal Marriage Act, he had to obtain the King's consent – which he had not – and thus the union was deemed illegal.

Prince George's younger brother, the Duke of York, had married in 1791 with George III's approval. The Duke had been studying the principles of military strategy in Prussia when he encountered Princess Frederica of Prussia in the summer of 1789. She had brought to the field a carriage stuffed with sausage, tongue and a good supply of wine – perhaps anticipating a royal appetite. At this enormous military picnic, the Duke of York was her best customer and a romance soon blossomed. Two

years later, the Duke presented the Princess with a bouquet of flowers, a ring and a thimble set with diamonds. In November 1791, the *Gentleman's Magazine* reported on their marriage, which took place in Germany.

Into the White Hall of the castle of Mecklenburg the Duke led his bride. He wore the full dress uniform of an English general, with scarlet coat and white breeches. She was dressed in 'a court dress of silver decorated with diamonds'.

The ceremony was performed according to the rites of the Reformed Church. Following the service, everyone retired to play cards before attending a state banquet at which court regulations were extended to the precedence of even those carving the meats.

When the couple arrived in England a little over a month later, a ceremony of remarriage was performed at which the Archbishop of Canterbury and the Bishop of London officiated. The Prince of Wales gave the bride – his new sister-in-law – away.

On this occasion the Duchess wore a white satin dress, decorated with tassels, a fringe of gold with 'a number of diamonds' and a court headdress of feathers. Once more the Duke of York – setting, albeit unconsciously, the pattern for many future royal weddings – wore the full dress uniform of a general in the Army. The Prince of Wales appeared in a court suit of chocolate-coloured fabric while the Duke of Clarence wore full naval dress.

It is at this remarriage ceremony that the first clear descriptions were transcribed of the male principals wearing the uniform of the Army and Navy. So common is this manner of dress today that it passes almost without remark: the groom's dress outshone by the bride's. Consequently 1791 was an

OPPOSITE PAGE: *Frederica, Duchess of York. Portrait by P. Strochling. The attendant dogs are perhaps reference to her love of animals, and her private zoo. (Reproduced by gracious permission of Her Majesty The Queen)*

BELOW: *Frederick, Duke of York, second son of George III. He married Frederica of Prussia in 1791, and began the practice of royal grooms wearing uniform to their weddings. (The Mansell Collection)*

His ROYAL HIGHNESS the
DUKE of YORK
Commander in Chief
of the British and Hanoverian Troops

important date for the development of male dress at royal weddings.

It is not difficult to see where the inspiration for the uniformed groom and attendants came from. Britain had embarked on a long series of wars against revolutionary and Napoleonic France which would not end until 1815. Military and naval uniforms had become a commonplace sight in the streets; moreover, while in the past it had been thought not quite acceptable to wear a uniform, even if one were a serving officer (uniform dress being identified as a form of livery and thus appropriate only for servants), in the closing decade of the eighteenth century an explosion of uniform attire occurred. With the beginning of nationalism, generated by the revolution in France, the need to identify national armies and navies became increasingly important. The style of uniforms, especially for officers reflected, too, the romantic movement in dress and the decorative arts. Thus the tradition of uniforms for royal weddings was born.

The Prince of Wales was obsessed with clothes and uniforms. They were a way in which he could express his extravagant personality and he designed the uniforms for his own regiment, the Prince of Wales' Hussars, created under the influence of Eastern European costume and the romantic images conjured up by contemporary artists. It had been his penchant for lavish clothing and various other luxurious temptations, that placed him in the position of requiring a wife.

George had heard favourable reports of Princess Caroline of Brunswick and had fixed his attentions on her. His mother, Queen Charlotte, was less impressed; through the grapevine she heard that the young Princess had to be chaperoned even on the dance floor, lest she make indecent conversation with the young men she encountered. Despite her misgivings, a marriage was agreed upon in principle and the Earl of Malmesbury, an experienced diplomat, was sent to Brunswick to conclude matters and escort the Princess to England.

Although versed in the language of diplomacy the Earl confided his private thoughts to his journal which, as a result, provides a fascinating insight into the process of acquiring a wife for an eighteenth-century British prince.

Corbould delin.t   Warren sculp.t

His Royal Highness Prince Frederick,

DUKE OF YORK, BISHOP OF OSNABURGH,

EARL of ULSTER, &c.

Publish'd as the Act directs Dec.r 17. 1791 by W. & I. Stratford N.o 112 Holborn Hill.

On his first encounter with the prospective bride he found a princess with 'a pretty face – her figure not graceful – fine eyes . . . tolerable teeth, but going'. The longer he stayed at Brunswick, the less this 'curate's egg' of a princess impressed Malmesbury. Although he had initially felt certain she would improve with closer acquaintance, he realized that her awkwardness and impetuosity were considerable drawbacks. He advised that she keep 'perfect silence on all subjects for six months after her arrival in England' and repeatedly impressed upon her the importance of delicacy in language and manners. Aware of the Prince's legendary fastidiousness, he discreetly enquired about the Princess's habits of hygiene, and impressed upon her ladies the necessity of ensuring that their charge washed all over – and made less of a virtue of speedy dressing.

Attempts were made to improve the appearance of the Princess. In England, a tailor's dummy was made up to her measurements and Queen Charlotte interviewed two court dressmakers, Mrs Beauvey and Mrs Spilsbury, at Buckingham Palace. They made up a number of dresses which were then shipped out to Brunswick. Malmesbury reported to his master, the Prince of Wales, that 'it is amazing how well they become her'.

OPPOSITE PAGE: *The Duke of York in a general's uniform. He met his wife, a Prussian princess, while studying military strategy in Germany, in 1789. (The Mansell Collection)*

TOP RIGHT: *Frederick, Duke of York. Portrait by Sir Joshua Reynolds. He is wearing his Garter robes and the elaborate underdress of the Order. (Reproduced by gracious permission of Her Majesty The Queen).* RIGHT: *Caroline of Brunswick. (The Mansell Collection)*

Malmesbury's next responsibility was to escort the Princess on the long journey to England from Brunswick, through a continent at war, and in the grips of one of the worst winters in living memory. Even his recollections of a posting to Russia did not prepare the Earl for the conditions he encountered. Those of the party obliged to walk beside the carriages were in danger of freezing to death, and the Princess complained bitterly throughout.

In early April 1795 they reached Holland and soon set sail for England, transferring to the yacht *Jupiter* for the journey from Gravesend to Greenwich. Caroline arrived there at noon on Sunday, 5 April, four days before the wedding. It was then that the first real indications of the troubles that lay ahead were encountered, in the person of Lady Jersey, one of the Prince's mistresses. There and then she insisted that the Princess change her white muslin gown, worn with a blue satin underskirt, for a white satin dress and overmantle of green satin, trimmed with gold loops and tassels. She then kept the party waiting for an hour by arguing over the place allotted to her in the carriages that were to take the Princess and her attendants to London.

It was, perhaps, not the most relaxed and happy bride that met her husband two hours later in the Duke of Cumberland's apartments in St James's Palace. It was this first sight of Caroline that prompted the Prince of Wales to utter his exclamation of disbelief and request for brandy. When Malmesbury suggested water, George walked off to see his father.

His prospective wife was equally unimpressed. 'My God,' she said, 'is the Prince always like that? I find him very fat, and nothing like as handsome as his portrait'.

Despite mutual disillusionment, matters had proceeded too far for anything to stop the wedding. The Chapel Royal at St James's had been, according to the *Gentleman's Magazine*, 'most superbly fitted up and papered in a style to imitate crimson velvet'. The Lord Chamberlain's Office had organized the ceremonial and had the order of processions printed. Caroline would be escorted by the Prince's younger brother, the Duke of Clarence, accompanied by drums and trumpets and followed by the

Master of Ceremonies, a Gentleman Usher and two heralds, the Vice Chamberlain and Lord Chamberlain – a pattern established decades earlier. Caroline was not to wear court dress but the royal robes. Some months before Queen Charlotte had asked her son his opinion on the matter of his wife's dress. He considered and replied, 'I own I should prefer her being married in robes'.

The nuptial habit was described as a royal robe with a silver tissue petticoat decorated with silver tassels. The body and the train were also of silver, festooned on either side with large tassels, and the sleeves were embellished with lace and embroidered with feathers, perhaps in the form of the Prince of Wales' crest. The mantle of state – crimson velvet with silver tassels and trimmed with ermine – was worn over this dress. Upon her head Caroline wore the coronet of the Princess of Wales.

Four attendants, all in white, carried her train. They were Miss Colman, Miss Poyntz, Miss Erskine and Miss Bruhl. They were followed by the bridesmaids who were spared the labour of supporting the mantle, and were of greater social precedence than the others. As required by tradition, all were daughters of dukes or earls, and they were Lady Mary Osborne, Lady Charlotte Spencer, Lady Caroline Villiers and Lady Charlotte Legge. They all wore dresses consisting of a crêpe petticoat embroidered with silver spangles, stripes of silver foil with a fringe, and tassels in silver. An elegant train was trimmed with silver cord and tassels. Their hair was decorated with feathers in the form of the crest of the Prince of Wales.

White and silver were once more the emblematic and appropriate virginal colours for the bride, a tradition that stretched as far back at least as the marriage of George II's children.

The procession of the Prince followed the bride and her attendants. He wore a court suit with the Collar of the Garter, and was supported by the bachelor dukes of Bedford and Roxborough. The King and Queen came next, he also wearing the Collar of the Garter and the Queen in a silver tissue petticoat, decorated with white and gold embroidery and further ornamented with a laurel motif in green and silver. Her dress was of gold tissue, as was the train, which was trimmed to match.

OPPOSITE PAGE: *The Prince and Princess of Wales portrayed, perhaps inaccurately, as a happy couple. (The Mansell Collection)*

THIS PAGE, LEFT: *The Prince of Wales dreams that his marriage to Princess Caroline of Brunswick will rescue him from debt. Cartoon by Gillray. (The Mansell Collection)*

The Queen's eldest daughter, the Princess Royal, wore a dress worked in purple and gold, and festooned with a gold and laurel motif; the Princess Augusta had a train of silver, both dress and train patterned with flowers coloured rose pink and silver. The princesses Elizabeth and Sophia completed the royal procession, wearing matching crêpe dresses embroidered with white and silver wreaths of flowers.

The splendidly attired company observed the ceremony performed by the Archbishop of Canterbury and the Bishop of London and afterwards there was the 'Nuptial Drawing Room' – 'numerously and brilliantly attended', reported the *Gentleman's Magazine*. After a lavish supper at Buckingham Palace, the Prince and Princess retired to Carlton House.

There was no ritual viewing of the couple and this was, undoubtedly, fortunate. Malmesbury had observed the Prince carefully throughout the wedding. He had been very civil and gracious, but the diplomat knew this to be a façade. In reality the Prince was not sincere 'and certainly unhappy, and as proof of it he had manifestly had recourse to wine and spirits'. While the *Gentleman's Magazine* enthused about the marriage and noted that the royal family appeared delighted with the union and, in particular, the Prince choosing 'such a distinguished ornament of her sex, for beauty, grace and mental endowment, one in short combining every requisite to render her worthy of being the bride of the heir apparent' – and while the magazine described the brilliant illuminations in the city, the 'abundance of the fireworks and the tens of thousands of people who paraded the streets to a late hour, with not the smallest accident taking place' – Malmesbury knew better.

At the end of the long account describing his mission to negotiate the marriage treaty, to bring the Princess to England and to finally witness the wedding, he wrote, 'It is impossible to conceive or foresee any comfort from this connection, in which I lament very much having taken any share'.

Although the marriage began in disillusionment and ended with the bride on trial for adultery, there was one happy result. One child was born of the union: Princess Charlotte.

*L*ord Liverpool has the honour to inform your Royal Highness that he had communicated the drafts of the several papers and instruments relative to the marriage of Her Royal Highness Princess Charlotte with Prince Leopold of Coburg, to the Lord Chancellor who entirely approves of the general purport and will put them with as little delay as possible into proper form.

IN a dry manner Lord Liverpool was reporting on the progress towards matrimony of the Prince of Wales' only child Charlotte. The wedding was the cause of great family and national rejoicing and it was a suitably splendid affair. Its tragic end not only lent piquancy to the story but led to a rash of other royal marriages.

Princess Charlotte was born in 1796 and christened at St James's Palace on 11 February of that year. A precocious child, she was a great favourite with her grandfather George III. The hopes of the entire country rested with her when it became clear that the union between the Prince of Wales and Caroline of Brunswick was unlikely to produce further offspring. In order for the dynasty to continue, Charlotte had to marry.

In the early weeks of 1816, rumour that a marriage was indeed imminent spread across the nation. A Mr Vick was sent from Paris by the Prince of Wales to seek out Prince Leopold of Saxe-Coburg,

BELOW: *The marriage of George, Prince of Wales, and Caroline of Brunswick. Painting by B. D. H. Hamilton. (Reproduced by gracious permission of Her Majesty The Queen)* BOTTOM LEFT: *Princess Charlotte with her husband Prince Leopold. (The Mansell Collection)*

who had been identified as the most promising candidate for the Princess's hand. On 20 February, Leopold landed at Dover to be greeted by enthusiastic crowds, lining the streets of the port. Interest was whipped up by the expanding number of newspapers and an improvement in the general education of the population. Rising living standards led to a more articulate population which was eager to be entertained by royal events – in particular, weddings. Royal weddings were well on the way to becoming the media spectacles they are today.

Close inspection and reports of the groom were an early feature. For example, *The Times* observed of Leopold that 'his appearance is eminently calculated to make a favourable impression on Englishmen . . . this manly person [is] good natured and

diffident – his manners are simple, unaffected and unassuming'.

After nearly a generation at war with France and its allies, Britain was acutely aware of her national identity; in 1816 she sought a focus for national unity and a reaffirmation of the qualities thought to be quintessentially British. The royal wedding was to provide both.

In London, while staying with the Duke of Clarence, Prince Leopold faced the excited crowds. He appeared on the balcony of the Duke's apartments – wearing a blue coat, buff waistcoat, and grey pantaloons – to cheers from those assembled below. The marriage was to be a major court and national event.

The Chapel Royal at St James's would not be used; instead, the Prince's own residence, Carlton House, would have its crimson saloon fitted up as a chapel. A temporary altar, covered with crimson velvet was placed in front of one of the fireplaces and the special crimson cushions reserved for the Royal Family were brought from the Banqueting House in Whitehall, together with the six-foot-tall, gilt candlestands.

There was confusion about the bride's dress. Initially it had been assumed that she would wear the royal robe, with its distinctive mantle of crimson and ermine velvet. Rather late in the day it was discovered that these robes were not to be worn by the granddaughters of kings and therefore Charlotte would wear court dress.

For some time before the wedding, Queen Charlotte had given thought to the jewellery her granddaughter should have. She told the Prince that she had seen Mr Bridge of the Crown jewellers, Rundell Bridge and Rundell, and had examined stones. She had been shown a design for a necklace mounted in wax and composed of seven diamonds. Together with bracelets, also offered by the firm, the cost of the neck piece would be £3,152 10s – and with the larger centrestone which the Queen deemed necessary, the cost would rise to nearly £4,000.

While the Queen fussed about Charlotte's jewellery, the country's Prime Minister was concerned about an adequate financial settlement. Lord Liverpool had lived too long with the political effects of

royal debt – which fed the opposition's ammunition – not to take every opportunity to avoid possible financial trouble. He proposed that the Princess's allowance be increased from £50,000 to £60,000 on her marriage. This, wrote the Prime Minister to the Prince Regent, 'with due economy would enable the Prince and Princess to maintain an establishment suitable to their rank and station'.

The popularity of the forthcoming match may be gauged from the response to the advertisements placed for the positions of ladies of the bedchamber and in waiting; there were 574 applications for the first position and 279 for the second. The State liveries for the male servants were to consist of coats of bottle-green cloth, trimmed with gold lace, and worn with white waistcoats and breeches. An enormous spate of activity filled the palace in the months before the wedding. Even the carriages to transport the couple were specially built, while the estate of Claremont in Surrey was purchased as their residence. Three days before the wedding, on 30 April 1816, the Queen and her daughters inspected the trousseau of the bride. All of the dresses had been made by Mrs Triaud of Bolton Street and, in addition to the wedding gown, there were over a dozen dresses in rich and costly materials.

There was a dress of white net, embroidered in gold lamé over white satin, to be worn with a train of gold brocade inlaid with blown roses and trimmed with gold lace. There were several dresses of transparent net and of silver tissue with lace. There was a dress of 'India-worked' muslin, two of lace: one costing £400 and the other £330.

At Buckingham Palace, on the evening of 2 May, Charlotte was dressed in a gown that outshone all of these. Robert Huish, in his biography of Princess Charlotte published in 1818, believed the wedding dress to have been worth over £10,000.

Charlotte's wedding dress consisted of a slip of white and silver, worn under a dress of transparent silver net embroidered with silver lamé. There was a border of embroidered flowers forming festoons around the hem, while the neck and sleeves were trimmed with Brussels lace. The train was over ten metres long, in the same silver and white material as the underdress and ornamented to match. The jewellery she had been given included a headdress of

OPPOSITE PAGE: *Wedding dress worn by Princess Charlotte, only child of the Prince of Wales and Caroline of Brunswick. Her marriage to Prince Leopold was the occasion of great national rejoicing. (Museum of London)*

rose buds and leaves formed from brilliants, and a set of large drop earrings.

Dressed at a few minutes before eight o'clock in the evening, Princess Charlotte walked down the grand staircase at Buckingham Palace. On her right was Princess Augusta and on her left, an equerry, Colonel Stephenson. In the grand hall they were received by the Queen. According to Thomas Green, writing two years later, Her Majesty was dressed 'in a beautiful gold tissue'. Her gown was trimmed with gold and silver, with two flounces of silver net, embossed with gold lamé. 'The whole had a most novel, grand and magnificent appearance'. With her was Princess Sophia, whose headdress was 'a profusion of diamonds and feathers'. They drove in a carriage to Carlton House, with an escort of Life Guards clattering beside them.

Huge crowds lined The Mall. The Princess expressed surprise at the numbers who had turned out to cheer her on the short journey to her father's residence where, shortly after eight o'clock, they were received by the Prince Regent.

Following the trend established in the 1790s by his brothers, the Prince wore his full-dress field marshal's uniform, with the gold aiguillette on one shoulder, and a dazzling array of Orders of Knighthood.

They now awaited the groom. Prince Leopold had been staying with the Duke of Clarence. For his wedding to the Prince Regent's only child, he too donned military uniform. Although he was not raised to the rank until some days after the marriage, he chose the full dress of a general in the British Army. This consisted of a black two-cornered hat, a scarlet coat – the collar open at the neck to reveal a black silk stock – dark-blue velvet collar and cuffs embroidered with gold lace in a pattern of oak leaves and acorns, and an aiguillette fastened to his right shoulder. Beneath the coat he wore a white

waistcoat of fine cloth, the same fabric of which his breeches were made. His sword attracted particular attention for the hilt and sword belt were lavishly studded with diamonds and other precious gems.

Prince Leopold also wore the stars of a number of European orders of knighthood. These included awards from the states of Saxony, Prussia, Bavaria and Württemberg in Germany, as well as Austria, Russia, the Netherlands and Denmark, and the recently instituted British Order of the Guelph, of which he was one of the first recipients.

His splendid appearance was not merely designed to dazzle. It would have been interpreted by his peers as evidence of his service in the wars only just concluded against Napoleon and would have reinforced his image as suitable consort for a future Queen of England. Leopold was joined by the Duke of York, in field marshal's uniform, and his host, the Duke of Clarence, who wore the full dress of an admiral of the fleet.

In the first carriage of his procession was the Prince's lord-in-waiting, his secretary and an equerry. Leopold followed in the second carriage, with the ambassador from Saxony and Mr Chester, from the Lord Chamberlain's Office, who acted as assistant Master of Ceremonies. Clearly popular with the female spectators, the Prince had first to run an affectionate gauntlet of pats on the back while the crowd called down blessings on his future. The carriage horses were nearly led off by the enthusiastic gathering who appeared to want to pull the Prince to his wedding themselves.

The Prince found his way packed with cheering people and a band that played 'God Save the King'. Shortly after nine o'clock, Leopold and his entourage arrived at Carlton House. He waited with Charlotte in the closet, while the procession of the royal family, the Cabinet and the foreign ambassadors present made their way to the saloon. The Marquess of Hertford then came to lead first the groom, and then the bride, to the altar. She was supported by the Duke of Clarence who left her at the side of her father.

Charlotte was attended by five bridesmaids: Lady Charlotte Cholmondeley, Lady Caroline Pratt, Lady Susan Ryder, the Honourable Miss Law and Miss Manners – the latter being the daughter of the Archbishop of Canterbury who would conduct the ceremony.

Behind the Prince Regent, to the left of the altar, stood his brothers, the royal dukes of Clarence, York and Kent, with the Prime Minister and members of the Cabinet. On the other side sat the Queen, attended by her own household. Two crimson-covered stools were placed in front of the altar.

Her father gave Charlotte away. *The Times* later reported that not only did the bride advance to the altar 'with much steadiness' but that she went through the ceremony giving the responses 'with great clearness'. Prince Leopold was, however, 'not heard distinctly'. The final moments of the ceremony were almost overwhelmed by the artillery salutes of 'the brazen throats' of the batteries in St James's Park and the Tower of London.

Immediately after the couple were pronounced man and wife, the Princess kissed her father, the Queen and a succession of aunts, shaking hands with her royal uncles but, of course, since the Princess of Wales was not present, not sharing an embrace with her mother. She retired to change into a dress of white silk, with a satin ribbon and two rows of Brussels lace at the hem. For the drive to Oatlands, the country house of the Duke and Duchess of York, which had been lent to the couple for their honeymoon, Charlotte wore a *pelisse* of white satin, lined with sarsenet and trimmed with ermine. They left at about eleven o'clock and arrived at the house shortly after midnight.

The wedding was celebrated on an enormous scale. The ripples of delight spread out from the royal family to their immediate retainers and far beyond. As Thomas Green describes in his memoir of the Princess, 'Bride Cake' had been prepared on the orders of the Queen and it was distributed to all servants in all of the royal households. Meanwhile the Poet Laureate, Robert Southey, had dutifully composed some verses to celebrate the event and to herald the glorious future. He compared Charlotte to Queen Elizabeth:

And thus thro' future times should CHARLOTTE's *fame*
Surpass our great ELIZA's *name*

Following the austere, war-torn years, the people

OPPOSITE PAGE: *Carlton House, residence of the Prince Regent, where the marriage of Princess Charlotte and Prince Leopold took place. (The Mansell Collection)*

needed an assurance of better times, a monarchy untroubled by illness, and a Regency that was not universally popular.

There were particularly splendid celebrations in Weymouth, Salisbury and Bognor, this unlikely combination of towns having connections in common with the Princess. At Salisbury there was a grand ball, described as the most splendid ever witnessed in the city. There was a 'brilliant assemblage' of over 250 people, according to the *Gentleman's Magazine*. The dresses of the ladies, to complement the bride, were all of white and the ballroom was decorated with emblems and symbols associated with the couple and the royal family.

Throughout the kingdom, people were able to buy cheap commemorative wares of the wedding. In fact, the marriage of Charlotte and Leopold was the first royal wedding at which souvenirs were widely available. Developments in the manufacture of wares and, in particular, transfer printing in the eighteenth century, allied to better communications, meant that there was a growing market for items which could be produced on a mass scale. Probably the most widespread pieces were moulded jugs which featured the Prince on one side and the Princess, wearing a double string of beads around her neck, on the other.

At the centre of all of the widespread celebrations remained the Court. While balls and commemoratives took place for the common people of varying degrees, there were certain long-established court rituals that had to be observed. One of the most important was the 'Nuptial Drawing Room', the traditional get-together at which the bride and groom would be shown off to politicians, courtiers and diplomats; the royal family would receive the congratulations of the Court.

Princess Charlotte's 'Nuptial Drawing Room' took place on 16 May 1816, and according to Thomas Green, exceeded 'anything that has taken place in our recollection'. Certain of the arrangements were as for a 'Birthday Drawing Room' held, as the title suggests, on the anniversary of the monarch's birth. On 16 May, therefore, a guard of honour marched into the courtyard of St James's Palace preceded by the band of the 3rd Foot Guards. About three thousand people were said to be present, all 'very elegantly dressed', according to Green. Despite the fact that the Drawing Room was not scheduled to begin until two o'clock, the crowds began to gather at midday and continued arriving until four.

The Queen arrived shortly after two, wearing a petticoat of green and silver tissue, draped with blonde lace and ornamented with silver bullion, the hem additionally embellished with flounces of lace. Over this she wore a matching dress. The Princess Elizabeth wore white satin, the mantua trimmed with gold lace and the sleeves with Brussels lace and diamonds; her headdress consisted of ostrich feathers with a diamond tiara. Her sister Mary wore silver tissue and Princess Sophia of Gloucester wore silver lamé with 'draperies of magnificent silver, suspended with a profusion of jewels'.

At the centre of attention, the newly married Princess Charlotte wore a petticoat of silver tissue. The overdress was silver tissue embroidered with Brussels lace and her headdress a wreath of diamonds in the form of roses and leaves with an ostrich-feather plume. Green described it as surpassing 'all conception of the grandeur, magnificence, and brilliancy of its effects'.

The judgement on that dress might serve as an epitaph to the wedding as a whole. It had been the first royal marriage to be celebrated in England since the end of the war. Here was a country that had dominated the alliance of European states against Napoleon – the threat to long-established order. There was clear relief that the King's only grandchild was married to a man who represented part of that alliance; continuity seemed assured.

But that stability was soon shattered. On 5 November 1817, her medical attendants reported that the Princess had been delivered of a male child but that he was stillborn. Worse was to follow: a few hours later, to a horrified country, the announcement was made that the Princess herself had died.

With one stroke the succession to the throne of England was in peril. Clearly, the Prince Regent would have no more children. Of his brothers, the Duke of York had married but the union had not been entirely happy; in any case, the Duchess seemed more occupied with her menageries of goats, monkeys and other animals which she maintained at Oatlands. As prospective bearers of an heir to the throne they certainly would not do – there was a need for more marriages, and children.

In this way the popular marriage and much-grieved passing of Princess Charlotte contributed directly to what might be termed the *annus mirabilis* of Hanoverian royal marriages, 1818.

OPPOSITE PAGE: *The marriage of Princess Charlotte and Prince Leopold. The Princess is about to sign the register. (The Mansell Collection)*

— 3 —

HUNTING FOR AN HEIR

T HE early years of the nineteenth century, with the notable exception of Princess Charlotte's wedding, were not auspicious for the British royal family. The King suffered increasingly from bouts of mental instability and in 1814, the Prince of Wales became Regent – but he was ill-suited to play the unifying role demanded of the monarch.

His popularity was so sadly depleted that on 28 January 1817 his carriage was attacked and the windows broken by the London mob when he was returning from Parliament. His brothers were held in such meagre esteem that Parliament was reluctant even to grant increases in the allowances paid to them by the Exchequer.

After 1815 Britain went through a period of intense social unrest and economic difficulties. The National Debt had increased to a staggering £800 million and in 1816 a poor harvest brought misery to the working classes as the price of bread rose. Meanwhile, the government fuelled rising unemployment by releasing huge numbers of discharged soldiers and sailors onto the labour market. There were real fears of revolution and the Establishment continually perceived threats to law and order.

There was clearly a need for a strong line of succession; where uncertainty ruled there could be no assurance that the country would continue to have a royal family at all. The Prince Regent was no longer a candidate for fatherhood, nor was his only legitimately married brother, the Duke of York, able to produce an heir. Although the Duke of Cumberland did marry Princess Frederica of Mecklenburg-Strelitz in 1815, their first child died at birth two years later. The line of succession depended solely on the dukes of Clarence, Kent and Cambridge.

Contemporary observers could see this as clearly as the royal family. Peter Pindar produced a book of verse entitled *Hunting for the Heir*. It was a robust view of the problem:

> *Yoics! The Royal Sports begun*
> *I' faith but it is glorious fun*
> *For hot and hard each Royal pair*
> *Are at it hunting for the Heir*

The King's daughter, Princess Elizabeth, married Frederick VI of Hesse on 7 April 1818. There was noticeably none of the national rejoicing that had attended Princess Charlotte's marriage two years previously. Princess Elizabeth's wedding was an event essentially closed off from the real world outside of the Court; its magnificence confined to the witnesses at Buckingham Palace. Even so it was not untouched by the unrest amongst the labouring classes. Her new travelling carriage was not ready for the wedding, due to a strike by the journeymen employed in its manufacture.

One person who did witness the event was Richard Rush, the American Minister in London at the time. He arrived at the palace at seven o'clock in the evening to find cabinet ministers, other ambassadors and officers of the royal household in attendance. He was conducted up the stairs to the throne room – which had temporarily been fitted up as a chapel – where the ceremony was to take place. An altar stood in front of the throne itself, covered in a crimson velvet cloth and laid with gold plate from the Chapels Royal at Whitehall and St James's. Rush notes a particularly splendid piece upon which was engraved a representation of the Last Supper. At eight o'clock the Queen arrived. The Prince Regent was absent – an attack of gout and

OPPOSITE PAGE: *Edward, Duke of Kent. A career army officer, he considered it his patriotic duty to marry, and to father an heir to the throne. Oil painting by G. Dawe. (Reproduced by gracious permission of Her Majesty The Queen)*

THIS PAGE, ABOVE: *Princess Elizabeth, portrait by P. Strochling. She married Frederick, Duke of Hesse, in 1818. (Reproduced by gracious permission of Her Majesty The Queen)*

The Hombourg Waltz, with Characteristic Sketches of Family Da...

the painful memories of Charlotte prevented him attending a royal marriage so soon after her death. The bride had to be given away by the Duke of York. Supporters of the groom were the dukes of Clarence and Kent and they accompanied Prince Frederick to the altar where he waited a few minutes for the Princess. The ceremony was performed by the Archbishop of Canterbury and afterwards the Princess knelt before the Queen, who sat in a splendid chair of state to bestow her blessing upon

her daughter. Outside there was a forty-one gun salute in St James's Park.

Although the event was unaccompanied by any of the public celebrations that had characterized Charlotte and Leopold's wedding, in one respect at least Elizabeth's outshone it. Descriptions of her wedding dress and trousseau reveal far greater expenditure. All of the dresses were made by Miss Wing of 53, St James's Street, milliner and dressmaker to the Queen and the royal princesses.

London Published May 4 1818
by G. Humphrey 27 St James's St
nephew & Successor to the
late Mrs H. Humphrey

ABOVE: *A print illustrating the popular obsession with royal marriages, after the death of Princess Charlotte. (The British Museum)*

RIGHT: *Victoria, Duchess of Kent, by G. Dawe. A widow when the Duke of Kent met her, she was described as attractive and vigorous. (Reproduced by gracious permission of Her Majesty The Queen)*

The wedding dress itself was of silver tissue with two broad flounces of Brussels lace, each flounce surmounted by a motif of silver shells. The bodice and sleeves were trimmed with lace and the sleeves additionally looped with silver tassels. The head-dress was of ostrich feathers fastened with a bandeau of diamonds.

Elizabeth's trousseau consisted of a further forty-seven dresses together with various caps and bonnets. One dress was trimmed with pearls and blonde lace, another with flounces of Brussels lace. An elegant blue dress had a train embroidered with blonde lace and there were gowns of green and blue satin, muslin, kerseymere and cloth. From contemporary accounts it seems that Princess Elizabeth assembled about four times the clothing of Princess Charlotte.

P RINCESS Elizabeth was not really in the 'hunt for the heir'. It would be the male offspring of the King whose marriages would be followed closely for potential heirs to the throne. One verse of Peter Pindar's masterpiece was directed at the Duke of Kent:

> *That worthy Kent*
> *To couple soon is his intent*

For a long time the Duke had lived happily with Madame de St Laurent. His correspondence describes an almost blissful and certainly stable existence, 'we are of the same age, and have been in all climates and in all difficulties together; you may imagine the pang it will occasion me to part with her'.

From the moment he learned of Princess Charlotte's demise he knew that his future could not lie in the arms of Madame de St Laurent. Creevey, the famous diarist, had a conversation with the Duke soon after the news of Charlotte's death was brought to him. He said the event was more important to him than to any other member of the family since 'the country will now look to me to give them an heir to the Crown'.

Under the guise of a tour of Germany in early 1818, and with letters of introduction from Prince Leopold to his sister the Princess of Leiningen, the Duke sought out a suitable German Protestant spouse. He found a candidate in Mary Louise Victoria, widow of Prince Ernest Charles of Leiningen. Aged thirty-one, she was a mother and still attractive. Her sister-in-law, Louise, Duchess of Saxe-Coburg, noted that she was 'very beautiful, well-built, vigorous with a very white skin, black eyes and black hair'.

Having secured a prospective wife the Duke would need additional funds to maintain an establishment suitable to a married man. Increases in allowance had to be passed by Parliament and it was with great interest that he followed the debate. Funds were not automatically granted upon request

and the opposition seized upon the opportunity to embarrass the government, thus revealing the unpopularity of the royal family at the time. Many members were, however, concerned that the family produce an heir and after what was described as a 'warm debate' the vote was carried in the government's favour. The Duke of Kent returned hurriedly to Germany to claim his bride.

There was a quick betrothal ceremony on 28 May 1818 and two days later, at half-past nine in the evening, the Duke of Kent married Louise Victoria in Schloss Ehrenburg. The family assembled in the yellow-and-white state drawing room and then proceeded to the Hall of Giants, with its decorated ceiling, and walls lined with shields bearing the heraldic achievements of the House of Saxe-Coburg. The Duke waited for his bride under a canopy of velvet erected for the event. He wore his full-dress field marshal's uniform. The bride entered wearing a white silk dress trimmed with white roses and orange blossom.

Shortly after the ceremony, which was announced to the population by the guns of the castle battery, the couple set off for England where, in July, there was to be a double marriage with the Duke of Clarence and his bride Princess Adelaide of Meiningen.

Like his younger brother, the Duke of Clarence had closely followed the debate about royal expenditure in Parliament. He was dismayed to learn that Parliament had voted to reduce the money proposed by the government and in a fury told the Prime Minister that he would take nothing at all. In time he was dissuaded from this course, and his marriage to Princess Adelaide of Meiningen was planned.

The *Gentleman's Magazine* published a poem by the Rector of Teversal, which attempted to inject into the proceedings some element of popular appreciation of the dutiful unions into which the dukes were entering:

Again do Princely Nuptuals greet the sight
And Albion's realm around received delight
The Royal Dukes now take a blooming bride
May choicest blessings o'er each pair spread

May joys supreme long on their union shine
And Kings spring from the great illustrious Line

The wedding took place at the Queen's House at Kew, where an altar – specially extended to accommodate four persons at the rail – was installed in the drawing room. The room overlooked the pleasant gardens, so the additional work seemed worthwhile. The ceremony was, unusually, planned for the afternoon and the party assembled at four o'clock. The Queen took her place at the right of the altar, with the Prince Regent by her side. Other members of the royal family and of the household followed. The two couples were led to the altar and the Archbishop of Canterbury took the service.

The Duchess of Kent wore a dress of gold tissue with two borders of gold lamé in the form of scallops at the hem; each border was edged with gold trimming and the bodice and sleeves were decorated to match, worked with an additional pattern of Brussels lace. The Duchess of Clarence wore silver. The Queen retired to dine alone after the dual ceremony, while the rest of the party, led by the Prince Regent, sat down to enjoy what the *Gentleman's Magazine* described as a 'most sumptuous dinner'. At half-past seven the Duke and Duchess of Kent left to begin their honeymoon at Claremont, lent to them for this purpose by Prince Leopold. The Prince Regent invited the remainder of the party to tea in the cottage near the Pagoda.

The fruit of these weddings was not the line of 'Kings' for which the Rector of Teversal had hoped. The Duke of Clarence, who eventually came to the throne in 1830 on the death of George IV, produced from his marriage two daughters – one who died on the day she was born, 27 March 1819, and another named Elizabeth who lived barely a year after her birth in 1821.

By that time the Duke of Kent – who years before, had learned of a prophecy that he would father an heir to the throne – was dead too. Two years earlier, in 1819, his wife had given birth to their only child, a daughter described by Baron Stockmayer as a 'princess as plump and pretty as a partridge'. She was christened Alexandrina Victoria, and in 1837 she succeeded her uncle, William IV, as Queen Victoria.

OPPOSITE PAGE: *Queen Adelaide, wife of William IV. As Princess Adelaide of Meiningen, she had married William, Duke of Clarence, in 1818. Miniature by Green. (Reproduced by gracious permission of Her Majesty The Queen)*

— 4 —

ALL THAT IS LAVISH
AND SPLENDID

THE marriage between Queen Victoria and her cousin Prince Albert of Saxe-Coburg and Gotha took place on 10 February 1840. It marked the culmination of family plans hatched many years earlier. When the two royal babies were still in their respective cradles the Dowager Duchess of Saxe-Coburg and Gotha had remarked of Prince Albert, 'what a charming pendant he would be to his pretty cousin'. The intervening years had seen many changes in family circumstances, not least the accession of little Princess Alexandrina Victoria of Kent to the throne of Great Britain on the 20 June 1837, following the death of her uncle, King William IV.

Queen Victoria's initial 'great repugnance' to the discussion of her future marriage plans was utterly swept away in October 1839 with the arrival in London of Prince Albert '. . . who is beautiful'. Within three days of their meeting the Queen informed Lord Melbourne, her Prime Minister, that she 'has a great deal changed my opinion [as to marrying]'. On 15 October Prince Albert was called into the Queen's presence where, as laid down by protocol, she proposed to him. She later recorded in her journal that 'I said to him that I thought he must be aware why I wished him to come here – and that it would make me happy if he would consent to what I wished'.

With the date of the wedding quickly settled, Lord Melbourne hastened to research the protocol which had surrounded earlier weddings of a reigning monarch. While investigations reached back as far as 1554, when Queen Mary I had married Philip of Spain, it was the 1761 wedding between King George III and Princess Charlotte of Mecklenburg-Strelitz which was judged to be the most appropri-

ate model. The Queen, however, chose to diverge in several important respects from this model, especially in the matter of dress. 'Talked of wearing my robes at the wedding, which I wished not,' recorded the Queen in her Journal, following a discussion with Lord Melbourne. She chose instead to wear a simple but fashionable white silk satin court dress. The bodice had a low round neck, and short full sleeves gathered into double puffs. Edging the neckline, sleeves and the sharply pointed waist were narrow rows of piping. The fullness of the skirt was taken in at the waist in a series of deep forward facing pleats. This dress survives in the collection of the Museum of London.

A court train originally formed part of the ensemble and was made of the same silk satin. It measured six yards in length – in the estimation of the train bearer, Lady Wilhelmina Stanhope – and it had a border of orange blossom sprays, matching the garland the young Queen would wear round her head. The custom of wearing these flowers for weddings – traditionally thought a French custom – took hold in Britain in the early nineteenth century, superseding the tradition of wearing roses, as Princess Charlotte had done on her wedding day.

It was of concern to the Queen and to her advisors that the entire bridal ensemble should comprise materials of British manufacture. Accordingly, the silk satin was obtained from Spitalfields. Mrs Bettans, the Queen's dressmaker in London, had the task of making the dress, which was eventually trimmed with a spectacular set of English Honiton lace. The assertions made by 'a dressmaker', published in *The Times* on 8 February 1840, that 'Her Majesty's dressmakers and milliners are foreigners and no other find favour at Court . . .

OPPOSITE PAGE: Princess Helen of Waldeck-Pyrmont receives a kiss from Queen Victoria after her marriage to Prince Leopold, Duke of Albany, in 1882. (The Mansell Collection)

THIS PAGE, ABOVE: *Honiton lace veil and orange blossom garland worn by Queen Victoria for her wedding in 1840. Photographed some years later. (Reproduced by gracious permission of Her Majesty The Queen)*

Her Majesty's dress is to be made of Brussels lace instead of Honiton lace, though Honiton lace has been purchased as a blind', were entirely without foundation.

It would seem, however, that Queen Victoria had commissioned a large part of the lace she was to wear on her wedding dress many months before her betrothal to Prince Albert. This comprised a deep lace flounce to be made under the supervision of Miss Jane Bidney, 'lace manufacturer in ordinary to the Queen', and owner of a business in St James's Street, Pall Mall. Miss Bidney returned to her native village of Beer in Devon in order to better undertake her commission, employing there more than two hundred workers between March and November 1839. It might be construed that with the

ABOVE: *The wedding of Queen Victoria and Prince Albert. (Her Majesty The Queen)*

fortuitous completion of the flounce, at the point when plans for the wedding were growing apace, the Queen decided to order, in addition, sleeve flounces, a neck flounce, and a square veil to complete the set she required for her wedding dress.

This lace, the cost of which amounted to between £1000 and £1500, was of a very high technical standard. The striking design of scrolling foliage and large exotic flowers is attributed, following recent research, to the painter William Dyce and an associate at the Government School of Design in London. From early in his career Dyce had shown a great interest in industrial design and this example of his work amply demonstrates his great talents. He was himself to claim more modestly, 'they do much better things now; but for the time the Queen's dress was I think a great effort'.

It was Queen Victoria herself who undertook the design of the dresses worn by her twelve bridesmaids, each one the eldest daughter of a peer. On 3 December 1839 she noted in her journal, 'Drew and painted a little sketch for the dresses of my young trainbearers'. This 'little sketch' survives in the Royal Library at Windsor Castle and shows a white dress trimmed with roses.

At midday on 10 February 1840, amidst 'torrents of rain, and violent gusts of wind', the Queen's procession left Buckingham Palace for the Chapel Royal at St James's Palace, where the wedding was to take place. The route was lined with thousands of people who had clambered on chairs and even into the trees to get a better view. Many sported wedding favours which were, as *The Times* reported, 'of

ABOVE: *Detail of the Honiton lace flounce used to trim the wedding dress of Queen Victoria in 1840. (By gracious permission of Her Majesty The Queen).*
BELOW: *Detail of a panoramic view of the wedding procession of Queen Victoria and Prince Albert. (By gracious permission of Her Majesty The Queen)*

white satin riband tied up in bows and mixed with loops of rich silver lace. Others were merely of ribbon and intermixed with sprays of orange blossom. Whilst here and there were to be seen bouquets of huge dimensions of riband and massive silver bullion having at the centre what might be termed a branch of orange blossoms'.

As Prince Albert alighted at St James's Palace, it was observed that 'he was dressed in the uniform of a British field marshal and wore no other decorations than the insignia of the Order of the Garter'.

(This honour had been conferred on him on 23 January of that year.) He was supported by his father, the Duke of Saxe-Coburg and Gotha, and his brother, the Hereditary Prince. 'The Duke was dressed in a dark blue uniform turned up with red, with military boots similar to that worn by the Life Guards . . . the Collar of the Order of the Garter and the Star, and the Star of the Order of Coburg Gotha. Prince Ernest wore a light blue cavalry uniform with silver appointments, carrying a light helmet in his hand . . . the insignia of a Grand Cross of the Order of Knighthood'.

The Chapel Royal was crowded with guests, and while court dresses and uniforms were prescribed, ladies had been especially requested not to wear court trains in order to relieve congestion. *The Times* reported that 'There appeared to be an unanimity of feeling with regard to the total banishment of black'. At last, to a fanfare of trumpets under the direction of Sir George Smart, the bride's procession entered, with Lord Melbourne in his new full-dress coat 'built like a seventy-four gun ship' at its head. The Queen, her dress adorned with the Collar and Star of the Garter and a sapphire-and-diamond brooch, a gift of Prince Albert, was supported by her uncle, the Duke of Sussex, and followed by the flock of trainbearers. Hoping to overcome the difficulties experienced at her Coronation, when the trainbearers had become hopelessly tangled in their own trains, the Queen had decided that trains would not be worn. However, she also reduced the length of her own train, which was to be carried, and enlisted two extra helpers, so as Lady Wilhelmina Stanhope complained, 'we were all huddled together and scrambled rather than walked along, kicking each other's heels and treading on each other's gowns'.

It was barely fifteen minutes later when the guns boomed out over St James's Park to announce that the rings had been exchanged and, by five minutes past one o'clock, the procession had set out for Buckingham Palace, where the register was signed and the wedding breakfast consumed. *The Times* was careful to point out that, 'we are assured that not one of the cherubs on the royal wedding cake was intended to represent Lord Palmerston. The resemblance therefore pointed out . . . must be

Master of the Horse.   Mistress of the Robes.   March⁶ of Normanby.   Duches of Bedford.

William of Prussia. Tall and handsome, he was twelve years older than the diminutive seventeen-year-old Princess.

The wedding was to be a pretty and, above all, light-hearted occasion. Pink and white invitation cards were sent out to guests, informing them that the Chapel Royal had again been chosen as the venue. The 'rich robe of white moire antique' the Princess was to wear took the form of a fashionable court dress, made of materials of British manufacture, and put together by Mrs David and designed by Miss Janet Fife who received ten guineas for her pains. It was trimmed lavishly with Honiton lace, made up at a cost of £507 10s under the supervision of Mrs Eliza Darvill. This lace took the form of deep flounces, each having a design of bouquets of roses, shamrocks and thistles, within medallions. The flounces were gathered to the front of the dress under garlands of orange blossom and myrtle. The train, which would be carried by eight trainbearers, again the eldest daughters of peers, was similarly trimmed. The Honiton commission also included a square lace veil, which was suspended from a wreath of orange blossom and myrtle. Myrtle was used within the wedding flowers on this occasion as it is the traditional bridal flower of Germany.

Like Queen Victoria, the Princess Royal chose to design the dresses worn by her bridesmaids. *The Times* reported that 'they consist of a white *glacé* petticoat, entirely covered with six deep flounces

LEFT: *The wedding cake prepared by M. Pagniez for the Princess Royal in 1858. (The Mansell Collection)*
BELOW: *Photograph from an album compiled by Queen Victoria showing the wedding dress and train worn by the Princess Royal on her marriage in 1858. The dress worn by the Queen on this occasion was trimmed with her own wedding lace. (Reproduced by gracious permission of Her Majesty The Queen)*

purely accidental'. Little pieces of this cake were sent to the gentlemen and boys of the choir of the Chapel Royal in recognition of their services. At four o'clock Queen Victoria and Prince Albert drove away to Windsor. 'I and Albert alone . . . which was so delightful!' said Queen Victoria.

THE happiness Queen Victoria derived from her marriage, and the blissfully happy memories of the wedding day itself, caused it to be established in her mind as a model for the wedding days of her children. The similarities were to be most discernible at the wedding of her eldest daughter, Victoria, Princess Royal, on 25 January 1858. Her husband was to be Prince Frederick

V[?] [?] collection — 1858

over which falls a tunic of tulle trimmed with ruches of tulle looped up one side with a bouquet of pink roses and white heather. The body is trimmed with draperies of tulle with hanging sleeves of the same material trimmed with ruches. A bouquet of the same flowers is worn in the girdle and upon each shoulder'.

The feeling of lightheartedness extended to the thousands of spectators who lined the processional routes. *The Times* reported that they sported dress 'as befitting a bridal; there were so many white bonnets and gauzy veils'. A hundred and fifty people, all wearing court dress or uniforms, the ladies without their court trains, had crowded into newly installed seats upholstered in crimson with gold bullion trimming in the Chapel Royal. The men were allocated a square of twenty inches, the ladies one of twenty-four inches: 'The latter indulgence, however, as it turned out a most feeble and inadequate concession to the fashions of the day'. The crush was so great that, as *The Times* reported, 'a noble countess drops her cloak and shawl over the gallery rail onto the floor with a heavy flop . . .

another peeress looking over moults her feathers from her headdress and they come swirling down'. This was all to the amusement of the Queen, if embarrassing for those concerned, and polite laughter filled the Chapel Royal. It had been made abundantly clear to all that 'It is expected that no person will appear in mourning'.

O N 14 December 1861, Prince Albert died from typhoid at Windsor Castle. The Queen and the entire royal family were devastated, and the country was plunged into mourning. The calm and dependable Princess Alice, betrothed to Prince Louis of Hesse since November 1860, put all thoughts of her marriage to one side, as she helped to nurse her father through his last hours, and subsequently supported her mother through the terrible months following his death. The wedding was eventually rescheduled to take place on 1 July 1862 at Osborne House on the Isle of Wight. As Princess Alice informed Lady Eleanor Stanley, 'the Queen to be present at it in her widow's weeds and the whole thing to be as private as possible'.

Princess Alice and Prince Louis of Hesse leave Osborne House for their honeymoon at St Clare, 12 July 1862. (The Mansell Collection). BOTTOM RIGHT: *The wedding of the Prince of Wales and Princess Alexandra of Denmark, 1863. The Prince is wearing the robes of the Order of the Garter. (Reproduced by gracious permission of Her Majesty The Queen)*

There were few plans to be made as there would only be a small number of guests, few flowers, and the only bridesmaids would be the bride's three sisters, princesses Helena, Louise and Beatrice, and her new sister-in-law Princess Anna of Hesse. The dining room at Osborne, in which the marriage ceremony was held, dominated by the large Winterhalter painting of Queen Victoria, Prince Albert and their five eldest children, was newly draped with dark blue cloth. The male guests were requested to wear 'Black evening coats, white waistcoats, black neckcloths', while the ladies were to wear 'Grey or violet morning dresses, grey or white gloves'. Even the sprigged white net dresses of the bridesmaids were trimmed with grey silk ribbons.

The Queen, wearing black silk, and her 'widow's cap' – or 'sad cap', as the six-year-old Princess Beatrice termed it – was seated in an armchair, discreetly shielded from inquisitive glances by her sons, when the procession of the bride entered. She wore a 'half-high dress with a deep flounce of Honiton lace, a veil of the same and a wreath of orange blossoms and myrtle'. It was a simple style and not embellished with a court train. Queen Victoria later confided to her daughter, the Princess Royal, that the wedding of 'poor Alice' had been 'more like a funeral'.

D ESPITE the national mourning of the death of Prince Albert, it would have been difficult indeed to suppress the great public interest in the wedding of the heir to the throne. The almost suffocating grief of Queen Victoria, however, continued unabated. Her response to her daughter Victoria's enthusiastic support of the match proposed between the Prince of Wales and Princess Alexandra of Denmark was, 'Dear child! your ecstasy at the whole thing is to me very incomprehensible'. However, the date of the wedding was settled as 10 March 1863 and St George's Chapel, Windsor Castle was selected as the venue. The news was greeted with some surprise – the chapel had last seen a royal wedding (that of the Black Prince) in 1361. *Punch* commented wryly, 'It is now settled that the marriage of the Prince of Wales is not to take place in London, but in an obscure village in Berkshire, remarkable only for an old castle and non-sanitary arrangements'.

The Queen was to take no part in the ceremonial. Dressed in 'black silk with crêpe, a long veil to my cap and for the first time since December '61 the ribbon, star and badge of the Order of the Garter, the latter being the last one my beloved had worn . . .', she would walk alone to the closet of Catherine of Aragon, set high above the choir of the chapel from which she could privately view the proceedings below. Members of the royal family were informed that mourning restrictions were not

LEFT: *The marriage of Princess Alice and Prince Louis of Hesse, 1862. The venue selected was the dining room at Osborne House on the Isle of Wight. Oil painting by George Thomas. (Reproduced by gracious permission of Her Majesty The Queen)*

lifted, and lilac and white, or white and grey dresses would be required. Thus Princess Helena's white tulle dress, made up by Lewis and Allenby in London, was trimmed with lilacs. Princess Alice wore a dress of violet silk, trimmed with her wedding lace; from her shoulders streamed a court train of violet velvet trimmed with ermine which, as Queen Victoria explained, 'Beloved Mama had worn at Vicky's wedding'.

Matters were relaxed with regard to the dress worn by Princess Alexandra and she donned a fashionable court dress of completely English manufacture. It was described as a 'petticoat of white satin trimmed with chatelaines of orange blossom, myrtle and bouffantes of tulle, Honiton lace, and bouquets of orange blossom and myrtle'. A Honiton veil had been made up to match the lace of the dress, with its design of cornucopias from which tumbled roses, shamrocks and thistles. The dress was made by Mrs James of London. The

Princess was allowed eight bridesmaids, matching the number who had attended the Princess Royal. They were all the eldest daughters of peers. Another link with the earlier wedding was the inclusion into the wedding bouquet of a little sprig of myrtle taken from a bush grown from a sprig carried by the Princess Royal.

The event was judged to be most magnificent; it was reported that the Duchess of Westminster wore half-a-million pounds worth of jewels, almost rivalling the splendid garb of the exotic Maharaja Dhuleep Singh and his wife. Lady Spence caused a considerable stir when she arrived in a dress reputed to have belonged to Queen Marie Antoinette.

The royal procession was preceded by the dramatic entry of the Knights of the Garter, wearing their flowing ceremonial robes. However, as the strains of the 'Chorale' – composed by Prince Albert and sung by Jenny Lind – was heard, the comment made by *The Times* about the wedding of Princess

Service sheet for the marriage of the Prince of Wales to Princess Alexandra of Denmark in 1863. The late Prince Consort had compiled the music for the Chorale: 'This day with joyful heart and wife'. (Reproduced by gracious permission of Her Majesty The Queen)

black silk. In 1882, when Prince Leopold married Princess Helen of Waldeck-Pyrmont, the Queen resumed her practice, established at the marriage of the Princess Royal, of wearing her 'dear' wedding lace. She mounted it over black satin, however, on this occasion.

O NLY the marriages of Prince Alfred and Princess Beatrice diverged significantly from this pattern. Prince Alfred married Grand Duchess Marie of Russia on 23 January 1874. It took place in the Winter Palace, St Petersburg, and was the only wedding of all her children that the Queen did not attend in person. It was to take the form of a double ceremony; the Russian Orthodox service held in the chapel was followed by an Anglican service conducted by Dean Stanley of Westminster in the Alexander Hall. While the British

BOTTOM RIGHT: *The marriage of Princess Helena and Prince Christian of Schleswig-Holstein in the Private Chapel, Windsor Castle, 1866. (Reproduced by gracious permission of Her Majesty The Queen)*
OPPOSITE PAGE, TOP LEFT: *Sketch of Princess Marie of Russia's special cloth-of-silver Russian court dress, worn for her marriage to Prince Alfred in St Petersburg, 1874. Watercolour by Chevalier. (Reproduced by gracious permission of Her Majesty The Queen).* RIGHT: *Princess Helen of Waldeck-Pyrmont in her wedding dress. The dress was trimmed with point d'Alençon lace. (Reproduced by gracious permission of Her Majesty The Queen)*

Alice might equally apply: 'There was no concealing that the most conspicuous person in that place, on that day, was he who was not there'.

Following the wedding of Princess Alexandra and the Prince of Wales, Windsor came to be the preferred venue for the weddings of Queen Victoria's younger children. In the case of the marriage of Princess Helen to Prince Christian of Schleswig-Holstein on 5 July 1866, the private chapel within the castle was used, but on subsequent occasions, St George's Chapel was deemed more appropriate. One each occasion the daughter or daughter-in-law of the Queen would wear a fashionable court dress trimmed with orange blossom, and it became a tradition to include sprigs of myrtle grown from a piece carried by the Princess Royal. They were attended by eight bridesmaids holding with the custom of each being the eldest daughter of a peer. Young ladies of the Villiers, Wellesley, Hamilton and Murray families, amongst many others, would be called upon one by one to undertake this duty.

The dresses worn by Queen Victoria on these occasions gradually became more decorative. The dress she chose for the wedding of Princess Helena was black brocade with silver, and for the wedding of Prince Arthur to Princess Louise Margaret of Prussia, on 13 March 1879, she donned, in addition, a black velvet court train embroidered with

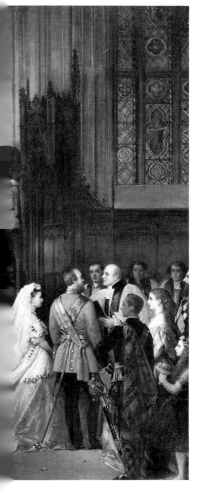

royal party – including the Prince and Princess of Wales, and Prince Arthur – wore court dress as appropriate in England, the ladies wearing plumes and trains if taking part in the procession, plumes alone, if they were not, the Russian court had its own distinctive style of dress. The sheer elegance and luxury of the Russian style of dress enormously impressed the many reporters sent by newspapers to cover the occasion. From their vantage point in the gallery overlooking the processional route through the Salle des Armes, lined with lancers with drawn swords, they observed the streams of court officials in ceremonial dress and ladies with 'long veils flowing over their silk and velvet trains'. There was a multitude of uniforms and an infinity of gold lace and sparkling orders. Many of the details of the Russian dress proved beyond the descriptive powers of the male observers. The traditional Russian *kokoshnik* headdress worn on ceremonial occasions was termed a 'sort of Marie Stuart cap'.

The bride entered the chapel on the arm of Prince Alfred, wearing Russian court dress. This comprised a low-cut bodice with long, hanging sleeves, worn with a stomacher that matched a lavish silver-embroidered petticoat and train. Over these garments a crimson velvet mantle lined with ermine was worn. Ornaments included a diamond collar and a crown from which hung a lace veil.

The splendour of the Russian Orthodox service could not be matched at the Anglican service later. However, it was reported that the Alexander Hall, with its newly installed velvet-covered altar and altar rails looked surprisingly like 'an English church'. As the bride entered on the arm of her father, she was handed a prayer book bound in white and a bouquet of purple and white flowers containing the traditional myrtle sprig, the gift of Queen Victoria. The service was read from the small black prayer book with large print which had been used at the weddings of King George III, Princess Charlotte and, most recently, the Prince of Wales.

THE wedding of Princess Beatrice, the youngest child of Queen Victoria, to Prince Henry of Battenburg took place on 23 July 1885 in St Mildred's Church, Whippingham, near Osborne House on the Isle of Wight. Recalling the melan-

choly atmosphere which had prevailed over many of the weddings she had attended, she, when aged six, had declared to the painter William Powell Frith, 'Oh no, I don't like weddings at all, I shall never get married. I shall stay with Mother'. Therefore, it was with some surprise that the Queen received the news that her twenty-seven-year-old

daughter had fallen in love with Prince Henry. For eight weeks she refused to speak to her 'Benjamina' and communicated only through notes. This intransigence was eventually whittled down by family pressure which argued that Princess Beatrice should certainly marry, if it were to make her happy.

The choice of a small parish church as the venue caused some consternation amongst the guests, especially with regard to what would be considered appropriate dress. The Lord Chamberlain's Office simply instructed ladies to wear *'demi-toilette'*. When no further clarification seemed forthcoming, the Duchess of Buccleuch issued the following statement: 'Ladies staying in the Isle of Wight are to wear long dresses with *demi-toilette* bodices cut down in the back and with sleeves to the elbow. Jewels to be worn on the dress and in the hair as for a full-dress evening party. Only the ladies who travel down to Osborne for the day are to wear bonnets and smart morning dresses. In case it may be of any help to you I will desire my dressmaker Miss Metcalfe of 111, New Bond Street to make my "body" at once so that anyone who cares to see it can do so by calling there'.

The Princess, who wore a dress of 'rich white satin with an entirely untrimmed train', was accorded the singular honour of being allowed to wear Queen Victoria's wedding lace. The skirt flounce was draped in two deep swathes across the front of the petticoat and caught up at the side with large bouquets of orange blossom. The neck flounce was gathered up to frame the deep V-neck and the sleeve flounces were altered to form short, tight-fitting sleeves, the edges caught together on the shoulder with a knot of orange blossom. On her head she wore Queen Victoria's wedding veil.

Rather than enlist as bridesmaids the eldest daughters of peers, Princess Beatrice preferred to select a number of small nieces to undertake this role. They wore simple dresses of figured cream silk, mounted over petticoats of machine lace. They carried bunches of pink and white carnations, the same flowers that trimmed their dresses.

Without her customary wedding lace, Queen Victoria wore what must have been one of the more innovative creations made up in her later years. It was of 'black silk grenadine mixture, double *broché*

OPPOSITE PAGE: *Princess Beatrice and her husband Prince Henry of Battenburg leaving St Mildred's Church, Whippingham, on the Isle of Wight, after their wedding in 1885. (The Mansell Collection)*

THIS PAGE, ABOVE: *Princess Beatrice was the only daughter of Queen Victoria to receive the singular honour of wearing her mother's wedding lace. The deep skirt flounce was mounted over the front of Princess Beatrice's dress in deep swathes caught up with orange blossom. The sleeve ruffles were inverted to form short sleeves. The lace was removed from this dress following the wedding, and survives to this day.* (The Lady). BOTTOM RIGHT: *Princess Beatrice and Prince Henry of Battenburg, with bridesmaids and supporters. Amongst the bridesmaids is the young Princess Alix of Hesse. (By gracious permission of Her Majesty The Queen)*

and double wire silk woven on a special loom at Lyons and destroyed afterwards so that the pattern could never be captured'. Amongst her jewels the *Koh i Noor* diamond was conspicuous.

Several of Queen Victoria's children took advantage of the need to commission dresses and accessories for their weddings to indulge their artistic talents. The Princess Royal followed her mother's example by designing the dresses worn by her bridesmaids. Prince Albert, who had demonstrated an interest in matters sartorial, decided that the designs for the lace to be made up to trim Princess Alice's wedding dress were 'so unmeaning' that he asked for another set to be prepared. Princess Louise was to design a locket as a present for each of her bridesmaids. It was made up by Messrs London and Ryde in rock crystal and blue and white enamel. In the centre was a wreath of roses and forget-me-nots which enclosed a scroll bearing the name 'Louise'. For the wedding of Prince Arthur, the royal family called in an artist from outside – the niece of Sir Joseph Paxton – to design the bridesmaids' dresses. They were to be composed of 'white satin *duchesse faille* and *mousseline de soie* embroidered with rose buds, and foliage flowers representing England, Scotland, Ireland and Germany.

The weddings of the British princesses – and Princess Alexandra as bride to the heir to the throne

– also provided an opportunity to boost native industries. Lace was to form an important part of all the dresses, and the small towns of Honiton and Beer, in Devon, were to benefit from the continuing patronage. A letter survives in the Royal Archives from Eliza Darvill, who had just returned from Honiton where she was supervising the making up of lace for the Princess Royal. She reported, 'the persons at work are most gratified at being employed for the Queen and are all striving to do their best'. Princess Alexandra, who had been given as a wedding present a beautiful dress of Brussels lace by King Leopold of Belgium, found it was considered quite inappropriate for use as a wedding dress. The dress she was to wear on 10 March 1863 was of English silk and lavishly trimmed with Honiton lace.

The sets of lace were to be much treasured by their owners, and were seen on occasions subsequent to the weddings. Princess Alice mounted her lace over the violet silk of the dress she wore to the marriage of her brother, the Prince of Wales. Princess Alexandra lent her lace flounces with their distinctive design of flower-filled cornucopias to

Princess Mary Adelaide, a cousin of Queen Victoria, for her wedding in 1866. The same flounces later decorated the dress worn by Princess Mary Adelaide's daughter on her marriage in 1893 to Prince George, the son of Princess Alexandra. Princess Helena's lace was worn by her daughter, Princess Marie Louise, for her marriage to Prince Aribert of Anhalt on 6 July 1891.

The English silk industry, centred around businesses located in Spitalfields, also received a boost in trade throughout the months leading up to a royal wedding. Before the wedding of the Princess Royal, Queen Victoria had made it expressly clear that 'the manufacturers of Spitalfields should be used as far as possible in the preparations of the dresses of the royal family'.

The dresses of the British princesses and their bridesmaids were made up by favoured dressmakers in London. Mrs David has been given credit for the dress worn by the Princess Royal and Mrs James for the dress worn by Princess Alexandra. This dress, however, was very promptly remodelled by Mme Elise of 170, Regent Street, who was to undertake many commissions for the Princess in subsequent years. The alterations had been undertaken so quickly that when the painter, Frith, asked for a sight of the dress in order to paint it accurately

in his ceremonial painting of the wedding, he was told it was too late – he was assured, however, that the 'Dresser promised to send you all she could'. This remodelled dress survives in the collection of the Museum of London. Mme Elise, whose business had achieved an early notoriety for being at the centre of a scandal concerning working conditions within the dress trade, was also asked to make up the dresses for Princess Beatrice and her bridesmaids.

The dresses worn by Princess Helena, Princess Louise and their bridesmaids were made up by Miss Unitt of 21, Grosvenor Square. The two weddings provide a pretty contrast. Princess Helena wore 'rich white satin with deep flounces of Honiton, the train of extra length . . . trimmed with Honiton guipure with cordons and bouquets of orange blossom and myrtle'. Her bridesmaids wore 'white tulle . . . trimmed with bullions of tulle and white *glâcé* slips, with tunics of silver tulle and chatelaines of flowers; forget-me-nots, blush roses and heather'. Princess Louise was attired in 'a dress of rich white satin covered with a deep flounce of Honiton point lace, trimmed with cordons of orange blossom, white heather and myrtle, and a train trimmed to correspond'. Her bridesmaids were dressed in 'white *glâcé* silk, trimmed with satin, and

BELOW: *The wedding of Princess Beatrice and Prince Henry of Battenburg took place in St Mildred's Church, Whippingham, in 1885. Oil painting by Caton Woodville. (Reproduced by gracious permission of Her Majesty The Queen).*

a tunic of gossamers and fringe, cerise roses, white heather and ivy'.

The construction of floral headdresses and bouquets for the majority of Queen Victoria's elder children had been the responsibility of Mr Veitch. He was later to be succeeded by Mr Nestor Tirard of Curzon Street, whose work proved so acceptable he was to provide all the artificial flowers and feathers, as well as quantities of brushes, for the trousseau of Princess Beatrice. It was Princess Mary Adelaide of Cambridge who adopted the most novel solution. The flowers worn at her 'Country Wedding', which took place at Kew Green, were provided by Kew Gardens.

The convention of patronizing British industry by royal brides did not necessarily extend to their sisters-in-law, brought up in other countries. Princess Helen of Waldeck-Pyrmont chose *point d'Alençon*, a French lace, as trimming for the dress she wore for her marriage to Prince Leopold on 27 April 1882. In the case of Princess Louise Margaret

of Prussia, who married Prince Arthur on 13 March 1879, the origins of her dress were made abundantly clear: 'the German Court Purveyors have again achieved a brilliant success and proved once more that German industry can still confidently compete with its foreign rivals'. The dress concerned was described in *The Times* as, 'A heavy white satin dress, a band of lace encircling the waist; the skirt was sewn with lace and decorated with a bunch of myrtle leaves . . . the train was 4 metres long and surmounted by a lace flounce . . . on which a sprig of myrtle was fixed'. The wedding veil worn by Princess Louise Margaret was of *point d'Alençon* lace, similar to that worn later by Princess Helen. Grand Duchess Marie of Russia wore traditional Russian court dress for her marriage to Prince Alfred.

The imaginative and luxurious dresses of the brides were the focal point of the royal weddings. The attire of their spouses did, however, attract some attention. Uniform was the favoured form of

ABOVE: *Pencil drawing of the wedding of Prince Arthur, Duke of Connaught, and Princess Louise Margaret of Prussia, by Ella Taylor. (Reproduced by gracious permission of Her Majesty The Queen)*

dress: only Prince Louis of Hesse had worn a black tailcoat for his marriage to Princess Alice, when the Court was in deepest mourning for Prince Albert. The uniforms worn by the British princes reflected their interests, and the close associations they might have to a particular service. The Prince of Wales, as bridegroom, wore the striking red uniform of an army general. His brother Alfred donned a naval uniform, though of the Russian service in deference to his Russian bride. Prince Arthur was to choose the uniform of the Rifle Brigade, his favoured unit. As a mark of their esteem to their colleague, the officers of the Royal Artillery had given to the Prince as wedding present a centrepiece representing a squad of artillerymen serving a sixteen-pounder gun.

Over their uniforms all of the princes wore a plethora of glittering Orders of Knighthood. The Order of the Garter and the Order of the Bath were most frequently found in conjunction with the family Orders of Victoria and Albert, and Saxe-Coburg and Gotha. In addition, Prince Alfred chose to wear the red ribbon of the Order of St Andrew to mark his honorary title of Duke of Edinburgh. Prince Arthur, marrying a young Prussian princess, added the Order of the Black Eagle and the Prussian family Order. The Prince of Wales had gone even further. As well as wearing the Collar and Star of the Order of the Garter, he wore the traditional flowing dark-blue velvet robes over his military uniform.

Uniform also proved to be the choice of the

German bridegrooms of the Princess Royal, Princess Helen and Princess Beatrice. Prince Frederick William of Prussia sported the garb of a Prussian general. The uniform was dark blue, embroidered with gold and, as *The Times* reported, had 'a gold aiguillette on the right shoulder, a silver sash, white kerseymere trousers. His Royal Highness wore the Collar of the Order of the Black Eagle and Hohenzollern and the Star of the Order of the Ducal Houses of Saxony of the Ernestine Branch'. Princess Beatrice's husband, Prince Henry of Battenburg, was mischievously termed by the Princess of Wales, 'Beatrice's Lohengrin' following his splendid appearance in the little church at Whippingham. He was dressed in the white tunic of the Cuirassiers, 'the epaulettes are rather large and of burnished gold whilst the helmet is of the same metal but on the top stands an eagle of highly polished silver'. Prince Christian of Schleswig-Holstein, who married Princess Helen, appeared rather more modestly in the uniform of a major-general in the British Service.

Of all Queen Victoria's daughters, Princess Louise was the only one to marry a British subject. Her husband, the Marquess of Lorne, was heir to the Duke of Argyll and the wedding was to have a distinctly Scottish feel. Many of the guests – as well as Prince Leopold and little princes Albert Victor and George, children of the Prince and Princess of Wales – sported Highland dress. The bridegroom dramatically entered St George's Chapel to the strains of 'The Campbells are Coming', wearing the uniform of the Royal Argyllshire Artillery Volunteers.

Preparations for each royal wedding began many months in advance. It became of utmost national concern that each bride should bring with her an extensive trousseau representing the best of native manufacture. For the Princess Royal, £50.18s.6d. was spent on dresses from Lewis and Allenby; £89.1s.4d. on gloves from Swears and Wells; £51.4s.6d. for umbrellas from Sangster; and a lordly £140 on fans from Alexandre. There were to be twenty pairs of galoshes and two drawers of sponges. Her sisters were to be similarly furnished. *The Lady* enthusiastically reported to its readers that Princess Beatrice would bring with her dresses

ABOVE: The wedding breakfast held in St George's Hall, Windsor Castle, after the marriage of Prince Arthur and Princess Louise in 1879. (The Mansell Collection). RIGHT: Princess Louise Margaret of Prussia in her wedding dress. The dress is a splendid example of German workmanship. (Reproduced by gracious permission of Her Majesty The Queen)

supplied by Mrs Stratton of Piccadilly, and Messrs Redfern. There would be dresses of tartan, Ottoman silk, and Irish poplin; dresses for tennis and for cycling. Hundreds of pairs of boots and shoes had been made up by Messrs Sparkes Hall of Regent Street, as appropriate for each ensemble.

More poignantly one might relate the details of Princess Alice's trousseau. £4000 was allocated for this purpose, and purchases of pretty colourful items were to be made under the supervision of Lady Caroline Barrington, Lady Superintendent to their Royal Highnesses the Princesses. However, following the death of Prince Albert, Queen Victoria was to remark sadly to the Princess Royal, 'I went to look at her trousseau and it is sad to see nothing but black gowns made up'.

For the foreign princesses, the matter of a trousseau was of no less concern. Despite taking advice from Lady Augusta Bruce, Princess Alexandra found her new wardrobe received unfavourable comment. No one could hope to match the opulence of the items prepared in Russia for Grand Duchess Marie, which were laid out for inspection in the Salle Blanche of the Winter Palace in St Petersburg: 'It is all that is lavish and splendid,

containing lace at 1000 roubles a yard. There are fifty dresses, exclusive of ball dresses, and exquisite furs . . . silks and embroideries are on a vast and wondrous scale'.

On a rather smaller scale, many local tradesmen were called into help with supplies needed to furnish the wedding venues for the comfort of the royal family and their guests. Great quantities of coloured cloth and garlands of orange blossom were regularly purchased from Caley's, the linen drapers in Windsor, to provide new draperies and decorations for St George's Chapel and the attendant retiring rooms. Mr Rimmel was paid five guineas to supply a fountain of perfume at the wedding of the Prince of Wales. More prosaically, the local chemist, Thomas Wooldridge, was asked to provide bottles of smelling salts and eau-de-cologne for the wedding of Princess Louise. And most mysteriously of all, the wedding accounts for Princess Beatrice include the purchase of twelve hip baths from Wood and Horspool of Newport on the Isle of Wight.

Following each of the wedding ceremonies, a celebratory breakfast was given for guests. The Princess Royal's breakfast was held in great splendour in the State Dining Room at Buckingham Palace but, following the death of Prince Albert, and with Windsor becoming the preferred venue for weddings, the procedure changed. It became customary that a large reception be held for the guests, perhaps in the Waterloo Gallery. Members

LEFT: *The marriage of Princess Louise Margaret of Prussia and Prince Arthur, Duke of Connaught, 1879. Oil painting by Sydney Hall. (Reproduced by gracious permission of Her Majesty The Queen).*
BELOW: *The marriage of Prince Leopold and Princess Helen of Waldeck-Pyrmont. (Reproduced by gracious permission of Her Majesty The Queen)*

RIGHT: *A wedding gift from the Duke of Connaught's friends in Ireland to celebrate his marriage to Princess Louise in 1866.*

Potage Julienne à la Royale
Pièce de Boeuf à la Flamande
Côtelettes de Perdreaux à la Marechale
Garnis de Gelée Moscovite à l'Ananas.

Pride of place on these occasions was given to the wedding cakes, which became considerable artistic as well as culinary efforts. The cake prepared by M. Pagniez, the Queen's confectioner, for the Princess Royal was described in *The Times* thus:

> The upper part was formed of a dome of open work on which rested a crown. Light columns on a circular plinth supported the dome and enclosed an altar on which stood two cherubs holding a medallion having the profile of the Princess Royal on one side, and one of Prince Frederick William on the other. Festoons of jasmine were suspended from the capitals of the columns and busts of the Queen, the Prince Consort, the Prince of Prussia and Princess of Prussia placed alternately.

Later it was to take Mr Ponder three months to build the wedding cake for Princess Louise. Her cake was five feet high and decorated with figures in sugar to represent the Fine Arts, Science, Agriculture and Commerce, as well as the more traditional roses, thistles and turtle doves! One might add this was not the only cake. Messrs Bolland and Sons had supplied another of very similar dimensions, as well as 'presentation cakes' for the royal family. '300 lbs of wedding cake for distribution' had been made by Gunter's in Berkeley Square.

At the end of the long day, each of the couples took their leave. Their honeymoon might take the form of a Mediterranean cruise – as was favoured by Prince Arthur – or simply a few days' rest before embarking on a ceremonial journey to a new home in a foreign country, like the Princess Royal and Princess Alice. The single old shoe thrown by one of the young princes after Princess Alice and her husband, as they drove away, had grown to a positive barrage of satin slippers by the marriage of Prince Arthur and Princess Louise Margaret. To the astonishment of spectators, a new broom was tossed after Princess Louise and the Marquess of Lorne: 'An ancient Highland custom'!

of the royal family were entertained separately. At the marriage of the Prince of Wales, however, the Queen chose not to join even this smaller select group, but dined privately with only the six-year-old Princess Beatrice for company. At Princess Beatrice's own wedding the breakfast was laid out in marquees set up in the grounds of Osborne House.

An extensive and varied menu was prepared for these occasions. Amongst the courses prepared by the cooks at Windsor for the wedding of Prince Arthur were:

La Pièce de Boeuf Glâcé avec Sauce Persil
Les Filets de Canetons aux Pois
Le Pain de Fois Gras à l'Aspic
La Meringue à la Chantilly
Les Soufflés à la Vanille
Les Puddings de Cabinet

This splendid repast almost rivalled that provided for the eight hundred guests of the Russian Tsar on the marriage of his daughter Marie:

5

VERY PRETTILY
ARRANGED

THE offspring of Queen Victoria's nine children were to number forty. While some died tragically young, from either illness or complications caused by the scourge of the royal family – haemophilia – among the survivors were those who married into royal houses throughout Europe. The interest Queen Victoria took in such alliances is testified in her extensive correspondence to all family members, in which she was helped by Princess Beatrice, her youngest daughter and confidante. In addition, the British public eagerly followed the swift succession of royal weddings during the last years of the nineteenth century. Even the details of foreign ceremonial were faithfully reported and explained in the popular press as Queen Victoria's web of influence spread wider and wider.

The greatest of this interest was to be reserved for the weddings of the children of the Prince and Princess of Wales, through whom the succession of the English throne would be secured. They had had six children, although the youngest, Prince Alexander, had died as a baby. Naturally speculation centred on their eldest son, Prince Albert Victor. After a series of unsatisfactory attachments, one to the Catholic Princess Hélène d'Orleans and a rejection from Princess Alix of Hesse, the royal family took matters into their own hands. Princess Victoria Mary Augusta Louise Olga Pauline Claudine Agnes, daughter of the Duke and Duchess of Teck, found herself the recipient of an invitation to Balmoral to be looked over by the Queen. Despite the Queen's disapproval of the rather extravagant lifestyle of her cousin Princess Mary Adelaide, the Duchess of Teck, and of the 'morganic taint' which hung over the family of her husband, their daughter

was found to be pretty, intelligent and sensible.

Prince Albert Victor appeared happy with the arrangement, and promptly proposed to the young Princess during a house party held at Luton Hoo. Princess May, as she was affectionately known, accepted him forthwith, and that night danced around her bedroom. 'Fancy it being poor little me!' With the wedding fixed for 27 February 1892, preparations commenced. Princess May selected items for her trousseau, including a splendid silk brocade with a design of mayflowers, woven up by Messrs Warner in Spitalfields, from which she intended to have her wedding dress made. Within six weeks, however, the Princess would lay her wreath of orange blossom on the coffin of her fiancé. Prince Albert Victor died on 14 January 1892 of influenza. Afterwards she retired, looking, Queen Victoria reported, like 'a crushed flower'.

Prince George, second son of the Prince and Princess of Wales suddenly found himself heir to both his father and the throne of Great Britain and his matrimonial plans assumed a national importance. Prince George himself had favoured a match with his cousin Princess Marie, daughter of Prince Alfred, the newly created Duke of Edinburgh. When she rejected his attentions his name was quickly coupled with that of Princess May. Although enthusiastically supporting the match, the families ensured that a period of time elapsed before an engagement was announced. Prince George, recently created Duke of York, eventually proposed on 3 May 1893. The Princess of Wales warmly congratulated the Princess:

God bless you and grant you all the happiness you richly deserve with my George and which

BELOW: *Albert Victor, Duke of Clarence, and Princess Victoria Mary of Teck. They were planning their wedding when he died suddenly in 1892. She was said to have been like 'a crushed flower' after his death. Photograph by G. Thurston. (National Portrait Gallery)*

was denied you with my darling Eddy. I am sure . . . his spirit is watching over you and rejoicing . . . that the clouds have been lifted once more from your saddened young life.

Queen Victoria recorded in her journal, 'I have so much wished for this engagement that it gives me the greatest satisfaction'.

Just a few days later, on 5 May Prince George met his grandmother in London to discuss plans for the wedding. It was decided that the date should be 6 July 1893, and that the bridesmaids should be the sisters of the groom, princesses Victoria and Maud of Wales, and eight little nieces following the practice established at the wedding of Princess Beatrice. In view of the fact that the recent funeral of Prince Albert Victor had been held in St George's Chapel, Windsor, the Chapel Royal at St James's Palace was chosen as the venue, despite the misgivings of the Queen, who considered it 'small and very ugly'. It would also recall for her the sad loss of her husband, whom she had married there so many years before.

Following the lead of Queen Victoria and the Princess of Wales, Princess May was to ensure that

materials employed within her wedding ensemble were of English manufacture. Having selected a second fabric design – consisting this time of silver bunches of flowers 'typical of Britain and Ireland', tied together with a true lover's knot, on a white ground – she took a keen interest in the manufacturing details as it was woven up again by Messrs Warner in Spitalfields. The dress was eventually made up by an English dressmaker, Linton and Curtis, of 16, Albemarle Street and it took the form of a court dress, as had become conventional. *The Lady* describes it as being of:

a very rich white satin . . . brocaded with silver . . . the long, plain train looked as if it were perfectly capable of standing alone, and just the front of the skirt was of white satin. It was edged with three tiny satin flounces trimmed with silver, and above these were three flounces of the beautiful Honiton point-lace . . . a trail of orange blossom on each side separated this satin front with its lace . . . from the brocade, and just above the top most flounce the other trails of orange blossom were brought from the sides, caught

LEFT: *Funeral procession of Prince Albert Victor of Wales, 1892. His fiancée, Princess Victoria Mary of Teck, laid orange blossom on his grave. (The Mansell Collection).* BELOW: *Group photograph of the wedding party of George, Duke of York, and Princess Victoria Mary of Teck. (Reproduced by gracious permission of Her Majesty The Queen)*

together in the centre and the ends fell to the bottom of the dress. . . . The bodice was of silver brocade with the floral design so placed as to form its sole ornament, with the exception of the Honiton point round the neck and the wreath of orange blossoms over it, with small bouquets on the breast and shoulders.

The wedding dress survives in the collection of the Museum of London.

The lace described in the account above did not represent a substantial new commission for the lace-workers of Honiton and Beer in Devon. Princess May wore arranged over her petticoat the flounces, with their distinctive pattern of flower-filled cornucopia, worn by her mother Princess Mary Adelaide for her wedding in 1866, and originally made up for the Princess of Wales in 1863. The wedding veil, claimed the Press, was also worn attached to a small wreath of orange blossom. It appeared, noted Lady Geraldine Somerset afterwards, to have resembled an 'elongated lappet'.

The Devon lace-makers were, nevertheless, resolved not to be left out of the wedding preparations, and they made up for the Princess a mother-of-pearl fan, the lace leaf worked with a design of cherubs and the cipher of the bride. The trousseau put together for her also included 'magnificent specimens of Honiton lace, purchased from Miss Herbert of Cathedral Yard, Exeter'.

It was, however, the rivals of the Honiton lace-makers operating in Amersham 'and adjacent hamlets' in Buckinghamshire, who provided silver lace to trim the dresses worn by the bridesmaids. The commission, under the supervision of T. H. and J. Muddiman of Tabernacle Street, proved very troublesome for the workers because of the short time allowed for the completion of the project, and the unseasonably hot weather 'which made their hands so hot that they dreaded tarnishing the silver'.

The Lady later described the dresses worn by the 'little maids' as 'short white satin frocks with chiffon flounces headed by silver lace, and the tops of the bodices were prettily puffed with chiffon under which the silver lace was laid. The sleeves were quite short puffs of chiffon; on each shoulder was a pink rose and the sashes were of white satin tied behind'. The dresses of the older bridesmaids were made of the same materials, but the bodices, trimmed with a larger-scale silver lace, had pointed basques and long sleeves. They were made up by Linton and Curtis, the makers of the bride's wedding dress. The silk satin came from Spitalfields at Princess May's express request.

Princess May carefully monitored the assembly of her trousseau to ensure that goods were obtained from a broad range of manufacturers. She claimed, 'we get trousseau things sent to us on approval from all parts of England, Scotland and Ireland so that we are nearly driven mad and have not a moment's peace'. Moreover she had been required to undertake the task twice, once following her engagement to Prince Albert Victor and then again for Prince George.

Messrs Redfern of New Bond Street, London, led the list of suppliers, making up Princess May's going-away dress of ivory-coloured Irish poplin, worked with gold cord and gold beads. They also

supplied dresses for walking, yachting and many other circumstances, 'with millinery to match'. Amongst numerous smaller purchases was a fine cream straw hat, selected from a number supplied for her inspection by the Chamber of Commerce in Luton, traditional centre of the British straw-plaiting industry. From Scotland came coats and jackets supplied by Messrs Scott Adie of the Royal Clan Tartan Warehouse, and as a special present from the Queen, a velvet robe of the Inverness Tartan was purchased from Messrs Romanes and Peterson in Edinburgh. The finest linen was obtained from Ireland both for lingerie and also for the household, from such firms as Inglis and Tinkler, and Robinson and Cleaver in Belfast. It was Mrs Sims, of 51, Dawson Street, Dublin, who undertook to make up 'ten lovely dresses, including dinner and evening gowns'.

Since the death of Prince Albert Victor there had been much popular sympathy for the young Princess, which was transformed to delight as plans for her marriage to Prince George were announced. She received many spectacular and valuable presents from civic authorities, specialist societies and private individuals. These included a diamond tiara from the county of Surrey, a diamond bow from the inhabitants of Kensington and an opal and diamond brooch from the Carpenter's Company. Perhaps the most unusual was the presentation by Mr Searcy of a spectacular wedding cake. *The Lady* described it as being:

> of two tiers supported upon silver pillars and adorned with trails of York roses among which are wreathed sprigs of maidenhair and asparagus fern . . . the royal arms and the monogram of the bride and bridegroom appear in several places. . . . At the top of the cake is placed a figure bearing aloft a posy of real flowers.

And, as Tsarevich Nicholas of Russia reported to his mother, 'Somebody even managed to present them with a cow'!

The crowds turned out in their thousands to witness the wedding processions, as they made their way under the triumphal arches, garlands and banners, which marked the route between Buckingham

Palace and St James's Palace on 6 July. 'The loyalty and enthusiasm was immense', reported Queen Victoria. At half-past eleven, the procession of the bridegroom set out; Prince George was observed to be wearing naval uniform, over which hung the Collar of the Order of the Garter. He was supported by his father and his uncle, Prince Alfred, Duke of Edinburgh. The procession of Queen Victoria followed, the Queen wearing 'in honour of the occasion my wedding lace over a light black stuff, and my wedding veil surmounted by a small coronet'. The greatest attraction, however, proved to be the procession of the bride.

The ceremony was witnessed by a huge number of guests crowded into the Chapel Royal; the gentlemen were dressed in 'uniform or full dress with trousers', and the ladies in 'full dress without trains or plumes'. To universal surprise, the chapel had been made to look very splendid. Decked with red and white flowers gathered from the gardens of Osborne and Frogmore, the chapel was hung with tapestries taken from Kensington Palace at the suggestion of Princess Louise. New ecclesiastical embroideries had been worked by the Art Needlework department of the Working Women's Guild for the sum of £22.10s.6d.

After the ceremony the company retired to Buckingham Palace where a wedding breakfast was served for four hundred guests. 'It had all been very prettily arranged,' concluded Queen Victoria, as she toasted the bride and bridegroom.

I T is interesting to compare Prince George's wedding with that of his sister, Princess Louise, who had married Alexander William George Duff, Duke of Fife, some years earlier on 27 July 1889. Princess Louise, at the age of twenty-two, had fallen in love with the forty-year-old Scotsman. Anticipating opposition from the family, she announced to her grandmother, Queen Victoria, that if she were not allowed to marry her choice, she would not marry at all. In the event Queen Victoria, admiring her directness, gladly gave her consent, happy that the Princess intended to make her home in Britain. It was a particular pleasure, she related in her letter of congratulation to the Duke of Fife, that 'my beloved grandchild should have her home in

dear Scotland and in the dear Highlands is an additional satisfaction to me'.

Popular interest in the match was widespread. The Duke was a wealthy landowner, a successful businessman and a much more acceptable choice than a German prince. As *The Times* explained:

At that time it appeared by no means impossible that the Princess or one of her children might one day sit on the British throne. In those circumstances a foreign marriage of the particular kind which then seemed intrinsically probable would have been frankly unpopular with the British people; who would have pictured themselves as being one day reduced to bringing back their Queen now wholly Germanized from some obscure grand duchy.

Whether or not she had this in mind, the Princess of Wales, commencing the preparation of Princess Louise's trousseau, was anxious to ensure that native manufacturers were thoroughly represented. *The Lady* applauded this thoughtfulness, explaining:

some most exquisite underlinen had been made by Mrs Ernest Hart's workers in County Donegal, some lovely Irish poplins have been ordered and a considerable proportion of the prettiest dresses have been made up in Dublin. Tailor-

made gowns and coats have had a prominent place in the trousseau and Scotch goods have been by no means forgotten. Our English jewellers have surpassed themselves in producing ornaments, and the young Princess will have as splendid a trousseau, all made within the radius of the British Isles, as would have been produced had Europe been ransacked for it.

Singled out for special mention later, from this splendid collection of dresses and accessories, would be many of the tailor-made costumes created by Messrs Redfern, and the poplin evening dresses from Mrs Sims of Dawson Street, Dublin, and Mesdames Berthe and Yeo of Portman Square, London. Hosiery and gloves were ordered in great quantity from Swears and Wells of Regent Street, and hats and shoes were purchased from Atloff and Norman in New Bond Street. As the Princess's future home would be in Scotland, a 'sweet little white lace dress . . . to be worn with a sash of McDuff Tartan' was purchased especially for wear at Highland dances.

The wedding dress worn by Princess Louise and the dresses of her bridesmaids were made by Mme Elise of Regent Street. Not only a well-established English dressmaker; Mme Elise was well versed in the demands such a project might make, having recently made up dresses for the wedding of Princess Beatrice. *The Lady* described the latest creation, again taking the form of a fashionable court dress, as:

one of the handsomest, and at the same time freshest and most proper that has been seen in London. The long train of white satin was absolutely without ornament, and finished off with five bands of the same material. The *point de gaz* lace on either side of it seemed to belong as to the petticoat of the dress rather than the train and gave a sort of unity to the whole. This lace was extremely beautiful and was laid row over row on the satin petticoat. . . . The front of the corsage was quite covered with lovely lace, and the elbow-length sleeves entirely made of it. . . . The little bunch of orange blossoms on the left shoulder communicated by a trail of buds and leaves with that between the satin folds on the right hand side of the skirt.

Having ensured that native goods were represented in the trousseau, it is interesting to note that the *point de gaz* lace trimming on the wedding dress, and that which formed the veil, was made in Belgium.

The design of the dresses worn by the eight bridesmaids – the sisters and nieces of the bride – later received mixed comment. Queen Victoria declared emphatically that they 'looked vy (*sic*) pretty'. By contrast, however, Marie Mallet, one of the maids of honour, stated, 'I thought the bridesmaids' dresses quite hideous and most unbecoming'. Breaking with convention, Princess Louise had chosen a pale pink faille as the fabric. They had 'demi-trains draped with *crêpe de chine* over which were arranged broad moire sashes'. All carried bouquets of pink flowers, with similar flowers adorning their hair.

Meanwhile, the Lord Chamberlain's Office had been working hard to ensure that the wedding day would go smoothly. One special task was to publish instructions with regard to dress. *Levée* dress was specified for men; for ladies, '*Demi-toilette*, evening dress' was the more ambiguous instruction. A small note on the printed regulations in the Public Records Office states, 'I am told this will convey everything to the female mind.' There is an additional rejoinder, 'I understand short, not very short sleeves'. The female guests did not, however, seem to experience particular problems with such information, perhaps recalling the helpful explanation given by the Duchess of Buccleuch at an earlier wedding.

The venue chosen for the wedding, the chapel of Buckingham Palace, also went against more recent practice. It had not been used since the death of the Prince Consort and had to be extensively renovated to make it fit for the occasion. As customary, the Archbishop of Canterbury was asked to officiate. The musical arrangements were settled with the help of Dr Jerkyll, the organist of the Chapel Royal. The bridegroom's and bride's processions would enter to Wagner's 'Marches', which had also been Princess Beatrice's choice, and would leave to Mendelssohn's 'Wedding March', a general favourite. Lady Llanover's suggestion that a Welsh harpist should play during the service was declined.

OPPOSITE PAGE: *Queen Victoria greets the Duke of Fife, after his marriage to Princess Louise of Wales in 1889. (The Mansell Collection)*

The Princess of Wales gave her son-in-law, the Duke of Fife, a green morocco leather dressing-case as a wedding gift. When opened, it formed a complete toilet-table ready for use, and contained a full set of silver-gilt instruments, brushes and mirrors, each with crown and monogram. (The Mansell Collection)

On 28 July, Marie Mallet set out early to admire the decorations in the chapel at Buckingham Palace, and found Princess Beatrice busily making last-minute adjustments. Outside, *The Lady* stated, 'each square inch of ground was occupied by an elderly but densely packed crowd . . . the lucky possessors of seats up on omnibuses [a penny all the way to Kensington Church] revelled on a free and uninterrupted sight'. They all eagerly awaited the processions from St James's to Buckingham Palace.

On his arrival at the chapel, it was noted that the bridegroom – wearing the uniform of the Banffshire Volunteer Artillery, a unit with which he had close association – was attended by a single best man, Mr Horace Farquehar, instead of the pair of supporters in attendance at weddings of the more immediate royal family. Princess Louise similarly broke royal tradition by adapting the popular custom of entering with the veil draped over her face. Queen Victoria – who had donned a 'not too mournful' dress of black and silver brocade, 'with quite a lot of white about it', though not her wedding lace – was somewhat taken aback: 'No pcs ever had and wh I think unbecoming & not right' (*sic*). Moreover, the Princess of Wales, wearing white satin trimmed with moss roses, was judged by Marie Mallet to look 'younger than the bride'.

Princess Louise, whose responses were somewhat inaudible, and who seemed to have 'a good deal of fumbling with the ring', was afterwards observed to 'simply beam with joy'. The company retired promptly for a wedding breakfast, graced by a splendid cake made by Gunter's. This confectionary masterpiece had been exhibited earlier to the curious at Gunter's headquarters in Berkeley Square.

The couple left for a honeymoon at Upper Sheen. Marie Mallet, who was among family and friends who waved farewell from the entrance of Buckingham Palace, remarked, 'the cheering was tremendous, I could still hear it a quarter of an hour after their departure'.

PUBLIC interest proved greatest in the older children of the Prince and Princess of Wales, but there was also an enormous curiosity in the fortunes of the many other countries with which the British royal family had become involved through marriage alliances. When a British princess became the bride of a reigning monarch, the public imagination was especially stirred – such events could provide an intriguing glimpse into the complex and even exotic court ritual of other European courts. The first wedding to provide such fascinating insight was the marriage of Princess Alix of Hesse to Tsar Nicholas II of Russia on 16 November 1894.

Princess Alix was the youngest surviving daughter of Princess Alice and Prince Louis, Duke of Hesse. When she was twelve, the young princess travelled for the first time to St Petersburg to attend the marriage of her sister, Elizabeth, to the Grand Duke Serge, the younger brother of Tsar Alexander III. Wearing a white muslin dress, her hair adorned with roses, and already showing promise of her later considerable beauty, the Princess encountered the seventeen-year-old Tsarevich Nicholas. Five years later, when he encountered her again, he recorded, 'My dream some day is to marry Alix H. I have loved her a long time'.

There were, however, serious reservations about the match on the part of both families. While Tsar Alexander III hoped his son would marry into a rather more prestigious royal house, Queen Victoria, suspicious of a Russian match, explained, 'The state of Russia is so bad . . . that at any moment something dreadful might happen . . .'. Tsarevich Nicholas, however, refused to look at either Princess Hélène d'Orleans, or Princess Mar-

ABOVE: *Princess Louise of Wales and the Duke of Fife on their wedding day in 1889. The dresses of the bridesmaids were of pink faille trimmed with rose buds. (Reproduced by gracious permission of Her Majesty The Queen)*

A carriage clock in the form of a sedan chair given to Princess Louise, and the Duke of Fife as a wedding present by Mr Charles Wyndham. It was manufactured by Messrs W. Thornhill and Co., 144 New Bond Street. (The Mansell Collection)

garet of Prussia, and they in turn refused to give up their faith for Russian Orthodoxy. Princess Alix rejected kindly but firmly the attentions of Prince Albert Victor of Wales, and Prince William of Prussia. In the spring of 1894, with failing health, Tsar Alexander III capitulated. He decreed that his son should represent Russia at the wedding of Princess Alix's brother Prince Ernest, Duke of Hesse, to Princess Victoria Melita, daughter of

Prince Alfred, and while there he had permission to propose. This task was undertaken on the day of his arrival and the following day the Princess accepted. Reconciled to the match, Queen Victoria declared, 'they are really so attached it is perhaps better so'. Tsarina Marie, equally reassured, wrote to her son, 'I can't say how delighted I am'.

While Princess Alix in England took instruction on the tenets of Russian Orthodoxy from Father Yanisheff, the Tsar's confessor, and endeavoured to learn Russian, the health of the Tsar quickly deteriorated. Although the marriage had not been scheduled until the spring of 1895, the Princess received a summons in October that she should hasten to the Crimea, where the Tsar lay dying. His death took place on 1 November 1894; the Tsarevich succeeded his father as Tsar Nicholas II. The following day Princess Alix was received into the Orthodox Church, taking the name of Alexandra Fedorovna. The wedding was hastily arranged for the week following the funeral.

On 26 November, the birthday of the Dowager Tsarina Marie, the many royal guests who had assembled to attend the funeral of Tsar Alexander III laid aside their sombre mourning. In a letter to her sister, Princess Alexandra recorded her ambivalent feelings to this tradition:

One day in deep mourning . . . the next in smartest clothes being married . . . such was my entry into Russia. . . . Our marriage seemed to be a mere continuation of the masses for the dead, with this difference, that I wear a white dress instead of black.

Charlotte Knollys, lady-in-waiting to the Princess of Wales, added, 'I am not sure that the wedding was not sadder than the funeral'.

Over the centuries the Russian Imperial Court had developed a sophisticated ceremonial ritual which extended to the marriage service. On the morning of her wedding day Princess Alexandra, therefore, found herself escorted by her mother-in-law from the Serge Palace to the Winter Palace through the crowded thoroughfares of St Petersburg, as a twenty-one gun salute was fired from the fortress of St Peter and St Paul. In the Malachite

ABOVE: *Princess Alix of Hesse and Tsar Nicholas II of Russia at their marriage in 1894. Princess Alix's heavy mantle is borne by court chamberlains. Oil painting by Tuxen. (Reproduced by gracious permission of Her Majesty The Queen)*

the traditional diamond nuptial crown on the Princess's head.

Princess Alexandra wore Russian court dress of the style Grand Duchess Marie had donned for her marriage to Prince Alfred. With a low-cut, close-fitting bodice, deep, hanging sleeves, a long flowing train – cut back to reveal a petticoat – Princess Alexandra's ensemble was of cloth of silver, lavishly decorated with silver embroidery. The extensive cloth of silver train was edged with a deep border of ermine, and over this was placed a Russian Imperial mantle of cloth of gold, lined and edged with ermine. A short lace veil was pendant from the diamond crown. As the Prince of Wales reported to Queen Victoria, 'darling Alicky has looked too wonderfully lovely'.

These robes proved immensely heavy. When the Imperial family and their guests had retired to the Malachite Room, Prince Ernest, Duke of Hesse, observed that his sister remained motionless and alone in the centre of the room. Without the help of train bearers she, 'was unable to make a step . . . she was almost pinned to the ground by its weight.

Therefore, it was with the assistance of many chamberlains, and Imperial servants rather than bridesmaids, that Princess Alexandra proceeded through the State Rooms to the royal chapel, accompanied by the Dowager Tsarina. She was preceded by at least one hundred and fifty scarlet-liveried court servants, gentlemen of the household, chamberlains and household officials, and the Marshal of the Court and his assistants. She was met at the door of the chapel by the Metropolitan, his attendant priests, and Tsar Nicholas himself, dressed in the red uniform of the Hussars, over which was displayed the Order of Hesse. Before an assembled company of guests – dressed either in uniform or the distinctive Russian court dress, 'the gowns being orange-coloured with embroidery' – and representatives of numerous royal houses, including the Prince and Princess of Wales and the kings of Greece, Denmark and Serbia, rings were placed on the couple's fingers by the Almoner of the Imperial Court. The nuptial crowns were then held over their heads by the bridegroom's supporters, 'Misha, Georgie, Cyrill and Serge'. Misha (or

Room of the Winter Palace, in front of the golden mirror of Tsarina Anna Joannova – before which every Russian Grand Duchess dresses on her wedding day – her hair was dressed in a conventional style with long side ringlets. On this occasion ladies of the Imperial family assumed the role of dressers, handing to her the crown jewels, which lay on red cushions. Baroness Buxhoeveden records that it was the Dowager Tsarina Marie herself who placed

Michael) and Georgie were brothers of the Tsar; Cyrill was his cousin and Serge his uncle.

Leaving the chapel, the Tsar and his new wife, again progressed through the State Rooms, before driving to the Anitchkoff Palace. They stopped amidst the immense crowds of cheering populace to pray before the icons in the Kazan Cathedral. At the Anitchkoff Palace, the Dowager Tsarina awaited them, bearing the traditional gifts of bread and salt. There was no other wedding breakfast, and no honeymoon. 'How I thought of Alicky,' commented Queen Victoria as she gave a loyal toast at a banquet held in her honour at Windsor. 'How impossible it seemed that gentle simple Alicky should be the great Empress of Russia!'

I F the reign of the Tsar and Tsarina eventually ended in tragedy, the reign of King Alfonso of Spain and his new Queen Victoria, almost commenced with disaster. Minutes after their marriage they were subject to an assassination attempt. Princess Victoria Eugenie of Battenburg, only daughter of Princess Beatrice, was to be the only other grandchild of Queen Victoria to marry a reigning monarch. The marriage took place in Madrid on 31 May 1906, several years after the death of the elderly Queen, when her son King Edward VII was on the throne.

King Alfonso XIII of Spain paid a State visit to Great Britain in 1905. Having decided his duty was to marry – but insisting, 'I want to love my wife' – it was rumoured that he favoured a match with Princess Patricia, the daughter of Prince Arthur. On his arrival in London, however, he found his attentions rejected, and his eyes were drawn to the fair-haired Princess Victoria Eugenie, affectionately known as Ena. Princess Ena recorded that she found the King 'very thin, very southern, very gay, very charming'.

In Spain public debate about the identity of their future Queen reached fever pitch. The prestigious pro-monarchist magazine *ABC* decided to ask its readers to vote for their preferred candidate from a list of eight eligible princesses. As results came flooding in, it became clear that Princess Ena was firm favourite, polling 18,247 votes. In January 1906, Maria Christina, Queen Mother of Spain,

wrote to Princess Beatrice asking whether an informal approach might be made to King Edward VII to gain his consent to the match. The King replied, 'He's a charming young man . . . I'm so pleased'. Before any engagement could be announced, however, Princess Ena had to be accepted into the Roman Catholic Church, by which move she renounced her place in the succession to the throne of Great Britain.

Preparations for the wedding could now begin in earnest. Again, an appropriate trousseau was required. Displayed to family and friends at an 'At Home', held by Princess Beatrice and her daughter

RIGHT: *Tsar Nicholas II of Russia with his new wife, Tsarina Alexandra. Their fate was sealed on 16 July 1918 when they and their children were shot by the Bolsheviks. (Popperfoto)*

at Kensington Palace, it was observed that it was dominated by pale pinks and blues, colours favoured by the young Princess. This was especially evident in the dresses prepared for her by Mrs Andrews of Portman Square and Mrs Batley of Ecclestone Square, London. Singled out for particular comment in *The Lady*, one of Mrs Batley's dresses was of:

> the very palest pink *ninon de soie* and it is trimmed with yards and yards of the finest *point-de-gaz* lace which was in Princess Henry's own trousseau and has been given by her to her daughter. At intervals on the *ninon* and apparently holding the lace in position, are sprays of raised and beautifully painted roses over foliage. It is indeed a robe suitable for a young Queen.

As well as the gift of lace from the trousseau of her mother, the Princess also received beautiful lace from Queen Victoria's priceless collection, which had passed to her daughter. In keeping with Princess Ena's energetic pastimes, sporting outfits, including 'a coquettish little motor cap of reindeer skins, and a Breton Sailor of white linen', were prepared.

On 24 May 1906 Princess Ena, her mother and younger brothers were escorted by King Edward VII to Victoria Station. A great many family members, including the Prince and Princess of Wales, along with diplomatic staff from the Spanish Embassy, and many Spaniards living in London, had congregated to wave their farewells. The cries of '*Viva la Reina Victoria*' commencing here would ring in the Princess's ears all the way from Irun on the Spanish border, where she was greeted by the King, to Madrid. Sir Maurice de Bunsen, the British Ambassador to Spain, declared, 'greater enthusiasm, and the more evidently spontaneous and unorganized I ever saw'.

As dictated by Spanish royal custom, a guard was sent to the Prado Palace – just outside Madrid, where the Princess was residing – to watch over her on the eve of the wedding. The following morning, at half-past six, she attended mass with her fiancé, a meeting which would have been considered most unlucky by British superstition. She later drove with her mother to the Marine Ministry building where she donned her wedding dress.

The English newspapers explained that by Spanish custom, this dress had to be 'made in Spain by Spanish people and was, with other dresses for special State occasions, the gift of King Alfonso . . . so for weeks a little army of work people had been employed in making the beautiful wedding dress which it is said cost no less a sum than £1400. *The Lady* described the dress as a:

> white satin *manteau de coeur* over four yards long, that hung from her shoulders with its silk embroideries of English roses and the arms of Spain surrounded by the Golden Fleece in pearls, and draped with twenty yards of Brussels lace. The gown, also of satin with embroidered roses, had a short *tabier* of Brussels point and the same lace was used on the square cut corsage. Sprays of real orange blossoms sent from Seville on the eve of the wedding appeared on the dress and also fastened to her fair hair.

Rather than wear a lace veil from her own family,

LEFT: *Wedding gifts from the Spanish royal family to Princess Victoria Eugenie of Battenburg on her marriage in 1906. (The Mansell Collection)*

OPPOSITE PAGE: *Princess Victoria Eugenie of Battenburg in her wedding dress. The dress, a gift from her husband, King Alfonso XIII, was made by Spanish needlewomen and was trimmed with orange blossom from Seville. (The Mansell Collection)*

the Princess – in view of the important Spanish alliance – was required to wear the *point d'Alençon* lace made up and worn by her mother-in-law, Maria Christina, who herself placed it over Ena's head. It was to be surmounted by a 'royal diadem of diamonds'. Diamonds also gleamed on her neck and corsage.

Meanwhile, the royal guests congregated in the Church of St Jeronimo in Madrid amidst 'the tapestries, the banks of flowers, and the perfumed denseness enriched by the coloured sunlight that pierced the stained glass window'. Spanish etiquette decreed that no other crowned head should attend the ceremony so countries were represented by the heirs to their respective thrones. The Prince and Princess of Wales attended for Great Britain. The fine mahogany State Coach bearing Princess Ena and the Queen Mother, and the Crown Coach – surmounted by two golden globes supporting the crown, and emblazoned with the arms of Spain and Naples – which held the King, made their way in separate processions through the narrow, crowded streets. The King, wearing the uniform of a Spanish captain general, arrived first and waited anxiously for his bride. Princess Ena entered the church an hour later. The service, at which Cardinal Sancha, Archbishop of Toledo and Primate of All Spain, officiated, lasted three hours. At its conclusion the couple returned to the Crown Coach for the hour-long drive back to the royal palace.

In the days preceding his wedding King Alfonso was aware that threats had been made against his life and that of his prospective wife. On the day of his wedding he had even made a casual remark about these threats, to Princess Alice, daughter of Prince Leopold, who was one of the British royal party. His underlying nervousness had, however, been apparent to all as he awaited the tardy princess in the Church of St Jeronimo, fearing perhaps that some incident had already taken place. More practically, he had ensured that the traditional throwing of bouquets of flowers at the royal procession was prohibited.

The prohibition, however, seemed to have had little effect, the Crown Coach was bombarded and in the narrow winding streets, the crowds pushed dangerously near. As the coach entered the *Calle Mayor* it paused momentarily due to the congestion. At that moment, a bomb concealed in a bouquet was thrown by Mateo Moral from an adjacent balcony. Despite Moral's laborious experiments throwing oranges from the balcony to check the timing needed to hit a moving target, he was unnerved by the coachman's hesitation. The bomb fell amongst the horses, killing twenty-four out-riders and spectators, and injuring over one hundred.

The royal couple hastily descended from the Crown Coach and took to the 'Carriage of Respect', an empty vehicle without decoration which traditionally formed part of a Spanish wedding procession. At this point, the new Queen noticed that her wedding dress and shoes were covered with blood. There would be no wedding photographs. The couple later presided over the banquet held to honour their marriage. *The Lady* remarked of the new Queen, 'her presence of mind and brave efforts to appear composed and even smiling were the subject of universal remark and admiration . . . and the tender solicitude of the courageous young King for his bride, were touching in the extreme'.

THE national pride that the above-mentioned alliances represented, the courtly traditions they illuminated, and the splendour with which they were undertaken, were reflected – if to a lesser extent – in the weddings of their heirs. The immense popular interest in the marriage of Prince George of Wales, whereby the British line of succession was ensured, has already been noted. But even when a grandchild of Queen Victoria formed an important alliance with another royal house, public interest was still intense.

BELOW: *A selection of dresses from the trousseau of Princess Victoria Eugenie of Battenburg. Dresses were made by Madame Lambert of Hanover Square, Mrs Batley of St George's Road, Nicholl of Regent Street, and Mrs Andrews of George Street. (The Mansell Collection)*

6

OVERPOWERING FINERY

IN the summer of 1880, the Emperor of Prussia, William I, decided that his grandson Prince William, eldest son of the Princess Royal and Crown Prince Frederick William of Prussia, should be found a bride. William was another Prince who favoured a match with the striking Princess Alix of Hesse, but whose attentions were rejected. Instead, the young man settled for Princess Augusta Victoria, daughter of Prince Frederick of Schleswig-Holstein-Sonderburg-Augustenburg, whom he had known since childhood. While she was neither clever, beautiful nor rich, she delighted the young Prince. As the Princess Royal related to Queen Victoria, 'Willy has written most touching letters (in his own funny style) about his great happiness'. The betrothal was announced at Baldesberg on 2 June. The date of the wedding would be 27 February 1881.

Like Princess Victoria Eugenie much later, Princess Augusta Victoria's entry into her new homeland was marked with great ceremony. On the day before the wedding, she reached Berlin where *The Times* records, 'All down the Linden the spectacle was most imposing . . . the houses on either side seemed literally to be tapestried with flags and carpets . . . triumphal arches raised on classical-looking pillars stood here and there all down the central avenue'. Forty thousand artisans, students and members of the trade guilds lined the route, wearing sashes, and carrying banners and trade symbols. As was their right, the Master Butchers of Berlin, wearing top hats and frock coats, rode at the head of the procession.

The royal coach, with its painted panels and large glass windows, was drawn by eight black horses with red harnesses, and accompanied by outriders, coachmen's pages and footmen. Within, the young Princess was seen wearing 'semi-evening dress', with a long train. On her arrival at the royal palace, she received a short address from Herr von Forckenbeck, Chief Bürgermaster of Berlin. As her fiancé relates, it was his duty, as it happened, 'to lead my company [Captain of the Bodyguard] through the Brandenburg Gate, along the route to the palace'. On horseback – with sword drawn 'at the head of his stalwart company of Grenadiers having peaked shakos of white metal and uniforms prodigal of gold and embroidery and trappings' – the groom dramatically appeared to greet his Princess.

Just before six o'clock in the evening the next day, the Emperor and other members of the royal family attended the civil marriage of Prince William and Princess Augusta Victoria, as required by law. The religious ceremony which took place in the chapel of the royal palace proved to be an immense affair. As *The Times* relates:

> The huge circular space was crowded with a dazzling multitude of generals, ministers, state officials, the diplomatic body, with ladies and officers in every kind of full dress, grave professors in their robes of office, princes, counts, barons and all the rest.

Following Prussian tradition, 'all the rest' would include palace servants, former nannies and fellow students.

Wearing the epaulettes of a major in the Guards, presented to him recently by his grandfather, Prince William entered with the bride on his arm. She was attired in a dress given to her by Queen Victoria. It was composed of 'white and silver brocade, and priceless antique lace clasped with flashing diamond

OPPOSITE PAGE: *Princess Margaret of Connaught with her bridesmaids. Her dress was of shimmering white satin, with very fine Carrickmacross lace, a gift from the ladies in Ireland. (The Mansell Collection)*

BELOW: *A postillion in the grand procession leading Princess Victoria of Schleswig-Holstein through the Brandenburg Gate in Berlin and on to be welcomed formally by the city. (The Mansell Collection)*

buckles, which supported trails of freshly-gathered myrtle and orange blossom'. The train was supported by four countesses – a Prussian custom. On her head she wore a lace veil and the crown of the Prussian princesses, which had earlier been placed on her head by the Empress Augusta in the Chinese Cabinet.

After the short, simple service, the royal procession left the altar to the sound of six salvos of artillery, which very nearly drowned the organ playing Handel's 'Hallelujah Chorus'. As decreed by Prussian protocol, there followed a 'High Court' in the White Saloon, at which the royal family received the obeisances of their guests. Supper was served in the Hall of the Knights, 'at a brilliantly lighted board groaning beneath the weight of massive gold and silver plate, banks of exotics, Venetian crystal and pyramids of superb fruit'. The company later reassembled in the White Saloon for the traditional *Tackeltanz*, as *The Times* explained, 'The Emperor and the bride and bridegroom and the Princes and Princesses returned and took their places under the Golden Canopy'. As the lights were extinguished, the doors were thrown open to admit the Marshal of the Court and twenty-four pages, all carrying torches. As music played, the bride and bridegroom rose and promenaded slowly round the room. On returning they took the hands of their parents and paraded slowly round again.

This procedure continued until all members of the royal family had been so escorted. Back in London, Queen Victoria gave a banquet in honour of the young couple in the Waterloo Gallery of Windsor Castle.

I T's interesting to compare the weddings of Princess Augusta and Princess Sophie of Prussia, the younger sister of Prince William. She married Prince Constantine, Duke of Sparta and heir to the throne of Greece, in Athens on 27 October 1889. Like her sister-in-law before her, Princess Sophie was accorded a ceremonial entry into the capital city of Greece on the day before her wedding. At her future mother-in-law's side, she drove amongst the crowds of spectators, escorted on horseback by the King of the Hellenes and his three sons, all wearing naval uniform. In procession behind her streamed carriages bearing the King and Queen of Denmark, the Prince and Princess of Wales, and the Princess Royal – now widowed, but wearing lavender rather than a more sombre colour. The entry was marked by a short, 'but most effective address of welcome' by the mayor, just as it had been in Berlin.

The wedding comprised a double ceremony, similar to that organized for Prince Alfred and Grand Duchess Marie of Russia many years earlier. At half-past ten, the bride drove in a golden coach, drawn by six black horses with silver trap-

LEFT: Prince Frederick William of Prussia. Engraving based on a portrait by Von Angeli. (The Mansell Collection).
BELOW: Princess Augusta Victoria of Schleswig-Holstein. Engraving based on a portrait by Von Angeli. (The Mansell Collection)

pings, to the cathedral for a Greek Orthodox service. The delighted onlookers were able to note her splendid white robes decorated with orange blossom. The Archbishop of Athens, with all his mitred *myrmidons* officiated at the long and exhausting service. Their stiff and heavy robes of brocaded gold 'made up a little for the church, which was otherwise undecorated'. The bride's supporters, her brother, Prince Henry, and cousins, Prince Albert Victor and Prince George of Wales, and the bridegroom's supporters, his brothers Prince George and Prince Nicholas, and the Tsarevich Nicholas of Russia, took it in turns to hold the golden crowns over the heads of the couple.

In contrast to the frost and snow which had greeted Princess Augusta Victoria in Berlin, 'everyone was suffocating from the heat' as the Tsarevich reported in letters to his mother. It was so hot in the cathedral that candle wax melted and fell on the shoulders of the people beneath. The ceremony over, the royal couple retraced their steps up the flower-strewn nave to the cheers of their guests; 'strangely enough to western ears', remarked *The Times*. The short Protestant service was held in the King's private chapel. Afterwards, the family 'starved and half-dead with the heat', went into breakfast. It was a modest affair, the large ceremonial banquet was not held until the evening.

WE have been much startled recently to hear of Missy's engagement to Ferdinand of Roumania, he is nice I believe, and the parents are charming – but the country is very insecure, the immorality of the society at Bucharest quite awful', recorded Queen Victoria on 2 June 1892. 'Missy' – Princess Marie, daughter of Prince Alfred – was quick, however, to ensure her grandmother's approval of the match, bringing her fiancé to Windsor for royal inspection (unlike her cousin, Princess Sophie, who had declined three such invitations). Though few words were exchanged at the meeting between the Queen, the young couple, and the Queen's Indian servant, the *Munshi*, all parties shook hands and retired happily. The date of the wedding was settled as 10 January 1893; the venue was to be the castle of Silmaringen, the birthplace and home of the Hohenzollerns.

Princess Marie was the first to admit she was a veritable 'daughter of Eve', with a great love of finery and jewels; however, even she was astonished by the 'masses of dresses, coats, hats, handkerchiefs, stockings, shoes and the linen' that her mother had commissioned for her trousseau. She admits, 'I with my sisters and many friends used to walk amongst them awed by their magnificence'. Princess Marie was given items which had formed part of her mother's trousseau earlier. 'Mamma had been extraordinarily prodigal giving many of her own magnificent Russian gems', recorded the Princess.

She had distinct and individual ideas about the style of wedding dress she wished to wear. She explained, however, that 'Mamma absolutely disagreed with these, and I was decked out according to her taste, and wore my rather overpowering finery as best I could'. This finery was to take the form of a dress of heavy white satin, with puffed sleeves, and a bell-shaped skirt spreading into a train. It was embroidered with pearls and trimmed with bouquets of myrtle and orange blossom. The Princess did win one point. She had a particular dislike of lace veils and obtained consent to wear tulle alone. This was to be kept in place with a diamond tiara, in which a small wreath of orange blossom 'lay curled as in a nest'.

The wedding comprised a triple ceremony, with Catholic, Protestant, and additional civil service – which, as in Prussia, was required by law. The chief Catholic ceremony was held in the cathedral in Silmaringen, connected by passages and walkways to the castle. The Press were astonished to find the church unadorned and in addition noted that 'the dresses of the ladies were almost without exception of a sombre hue'. It was not until the arrival of the royal parties that more colourful elements were introduced. The Kaiser, William II, looked particularly striking in the 'full dress of the magnificent Cuirassiers of the Guard; snow white, with huge gauntlet gloves, high shining boots and Lohengrin-like eagle crowned helmet'. Watched by Prince Arthur representing Great Britain and Grand Duke Alexis representing Russia, Prince Ferdinand – dressed in Roumanian military uniform over which the orange sash of the Order of the Black Eagle was displayed – awaited his bride. She entered on the

arm of her father, Prince Alfred, who wore a British admiral's uniform.

With this ceremony complete, the company returned to the Ancestor's Room in the castle, where congratulations were exchanged. A short Anglican service followed, at which the Rev W. V. Lloyd presided. He was a naval chaplain, a fact, Princess Marie remarked, that gave her particular pleasure, because of her family's close association with this particular service. *The Times* noted, 'special services were celebrated in the churches throughout Roumania yesterday on the occasion of the marriage at Silmaringen of Prince Ferdinand and Princess Marie'.

ABOVE: *Princess Marie of Edinburgh and her fiancé, Prince Ferdinand of Roumania. (Hulton-Deutsch)*

SEVERAL years later, on 15 June 1905, travellers on the 9.15 from Paddington to Windsor would notice the train was unusually crowded with 'Scandinavian ladies and gentlemen, the former fair-haired and fair-skinned, the latter in the best of humour'. The ladies and gentlemen concerned were travelling to attend the wedding of Princess Margaret, daughter of Prince Arthur, and Prince Gustavus of Sweden, which was to take place that day in St George's Chapel.

Princess Margaret was a lively, intelligent girl who shared with her fiancé a fondness for modern sports. She had a robust attitude to the compilation of her trousseau, as *The Lady* explained:

the Princess has seen more of the world, than the majority of royal ladies previous to her marriage and had learnt that the height of fashion is not always suitable to the individual and insisted on

LEFT: *The wedding dress of Princess Marie of Edinburgh. Marie chose to wear a veil of silk tulle rather than the customary lace. Pen and ink drawing by S. and H. Johnson. (Reproduced by gracious permission of Her Majesty The Queen).* BELOW: *Part of a silver-gilt tea and coffee set presented to Princess Marie of Edinburgh as a wedding gift by the Sultan of Johore. (The Mansell Collection)*

having everything that is most becoming to herself . . .

Princess Margaret was to select the young and innovative designer Pacquin for many of her dresses, which were made up in either soft shades of pink or blue, or dramatic combinations of black and bright green or blue. A great many of her dresses were trimmed with the products of lace-workers in Honiton, Buckinghamshire and Ireland. One particular lace, worked with a design of daisies, was especially favoured; Princess Margaret was affectionately called 'Daisy'.

Pride of place, however, went to gowns made up in Ireland, where the Princess had spent happy childhood years. She would arrive in Sweden with a fine collection of 'Irish homespuns and friezes, house and table linen, and lingerie'. Furthermore, the ladies of Ireland presented her with her wedding dress and veil. *The Lady* describes it as being 'of the softest ivory satin covered with lovely Carrickmacross lace in a design of Annunciation lilies, meadowsweet and shamrocks'.

The Irish associations also extended to the bridesmaids' dresses' worn by the Princess's three

ABOVE: *Princess Marie of Edinburgh in her wedding dress. (The Mansell Collection)*

eted position on the short processional route from the castle to St George's Chapel, witnessed the arrival of Prince Gustavus, at midday, wearing Swedish military uniform, and attended by his supporters, Prince Eugene and Prince William of Sweden. He entered the chapel to the march from 'Tannhäuser'. The procession of the King and Queen followed: King Edward VII in a field marshal's uniform, and sporting the Collar of the Garter, and Queen Alexandra in black-sequined net mounted over bright blue, they entered to Elgar's 'Imperial March'. With the company assembled, the bride entered on the arm of her father, Prince Arthur, who wore a field marshal's uniform, over which was displayed the pale blue sash of the Order of St Patrick.

The event was relatively informal, perhaps in keeping with the more relaxed protocol which prevailed at Scandinavian courts. The chapel was unadorned except for the fluttering banners above the stalls of the Knights of the Garter, and two vases of lilies, artistically arranged. It is interesting to note that only the sixty guests 'from the castle' were instructed to wear, 'Evening dress, *demi-toilette*' or 'full dress with trousers'. The main body of the guests were informed that afternoon dress would be quite appropriate. After the ceremony the couple departed to honeymoon in Ireland before travelling to Sweden.

T HE last of the major European houses into which Queen Victoria's grandchildren married was that of Norway. This did not, however, come about by normal line of succession, but by election. Since the early nineteenth century Norway had been linked with Sweden by a common monarchy under the House of Bernadotte. Sweden had traditionally been the dominant partner. By the end of the century, however, this union had become increasingly strained and Norwegian nationalism gained an increasingly firm hold. There were two alternatives: that the country became a republic, or that it elect an independent monarch. To bring about the second option, it was necessary to identify a suitable candidate for ruler. The popular choice was Prince Charles of Denmark. As second son of the Danish Crown Prince, he was not in

cousins and little Princess Mary of Wales, all of which were made of St Patrick's blue satin. The shade was matched to that of the mantles worn by knights of this prestigious order. The dresses of the older princesses were trimmed with graduated scallops of rich *point de venise* lace. Princess Mary's short frock had a single flounce around the hem, she wore a daisy wreath, and all the princesses held bouquets of daisies.

Public interest in the marriage was great and Windsor was 'set all agog' for a sight of the royal couple. Those who had been able to secure a cov-

and accessories were red and white. These gowns were made up by Miss Linton, one of the Princess of Wales' favourite dressmakers, at that time making for Madame Frederic at Lower Grosvenor Place. All the dresses were of 'white satin, the skirts embroidered with lilies of the valley, the bodices trimmed with frills of lace'. The dresses of the older princesses were trimmed with knots of deep red geraniums, and they wore the same flowers in their hair. The 'little maids' carried square baskets of red flowers and wore flowery wreaths to match.

While Sir Henry Ponsonby was to claim that £1700 had been spent directly on wedding preparations, surpassing considerably the £900 spent on the wedding of Prince George, the event was a modest affair. The fifty-five splendid plants which decorated the chapel had been only hired from Wills and Segal at the Royal Exotic Nursery and Winter Garden, Onslow Square, London. The Archbishop of Canterbury, who by tradition was asked to officiate, was requested to keep his address short. The reason for this restraint was the sudden death of Prince Henry of Battenburg, husband of Princess Beatrice, on 22 January 1896. Their daughter, Princess Ena, who had been selected as bridesmaid was unable to undertake this duty due to mourning requirements. Invitations to royal visitors and the diplomatic circle were to be restricted to those from Great Britain and Denmark alone. The ladies were asked somewhat ambiguously to wear '*demi-toilette* (square)', and the gentlemen, *levée* dress. The 'sad and downcast' bride entered the chapel to join Prince Charles, who was splendidly attired in Danish naval uniform and the Order of the Garter. Her responses throughout the service were scarcely audible.

Presiding over the whole occasion was Queen Victoria, who was seated in an armchair within the chapel, clad in a 'singularly rich dress and train of black moire antique embroidered with silver'. At the wedding breakfast held in Buckingham Palace, two wedding cakes made by Bolland and Sons attracted great admiration. These were the gift of the Queen. She was observed by spectators later standing by one of the windows to watch the departure of the young couple. They left amidst a

A cycling costume selected for the trousseau of Princess Maud of Wales. The young princess particularly enjoyed energetic pursuits, a pleasure she was later to share with her husband. Following their accession to the throne of Norway, skiing became a favourite sport, at which both acquired great skill. (The Lady)

flurry of rice thrown by the young bridesmaids.

Queen Victoria was fiercely proud of her family. Behind each wedding – whether it took place in Great Britain or abroad – her figure is ever-present. Under a benevolent and intelligent eye, matches were engineered and potential candidates for marriage inspected. The style and standard of each occasion was rigorously maintained to ensure that due importance was given to family tradition as well as ensuring that the customs of other states were honoured. This practice would be continued by her son King Edward VII.

OPPOSITE PAGE: *Princess Maud in her wedding dress. (The Mansell Collection)*

THIS PAGE, BELOW: *Princess Maud curtsies to her grandmother, Queen Victoria, after her marriage in 1896. Oil painting by Tuxen. (HM The Queen)*

— 7 —

GORGEOUS FASHION
IN PERFECT TASTE

IN 1918 the country emerged from four years of total war. Although many European dynasties had been swept away during these years, the British monarchy, led by George V, who had succeeded his father in 1910, proved more durable. All of the weddings examined in this chapter fall within this twenty-six-year reign — beginning with the marriage of Princess Patricia, daughter of Prince Arthur, Duke of Connaught, and a cousin of the King, in 1919, and ending with the marriage of his son, Prince Henry, Duke of Gloucester, in 1935.

The design of royal wedding dresses during this period followed contemporary fashion, which developed rapidly through these decades. The almost asexual profile of the dress favoured by Lady Elizabeth Bowes-Lyon in 1923, for her wedding to the Duke of York, contrasts sharply, for instance, with the close fitting gown made up for Princess Marina by Molyneux for her wedding to Prince George of Kent in 1934. Basically, the two dresses were, however, court dresses of their era, with a court train forming an essential part of each ensemble.

The uniforms favoured by many of the male guests in the congregation were also the regulation costume required by the Lord Chamberlain for court occasions and laid down in the various editions of the publication *Dress Worn at Their Majesties' Court*. Although the world of the early twentieth-century court remains far removed from our own, throughout the twenty years of peace after 1919 it was the focus of those who aspired to membership of good society. The train, one mark of distinction that immediately categorized a gown as a court dress, remained an important and con-

sciously designed feature in royal wedding dress throughout these years.

It is a special skill of the British monarchy to change, absorb the stresses of society, and evolve in a way that is pleasing to its subjects. Since the First World War, display at royal weddings has usually been in tune with what society has demanded. Elements that might have produced unfavourable public reaction were dispensed with.

There is, perhaps, no clearer contrast to be drawn between the way that the British monarchy manages these matters, and the practices elsewhere in Europe, than in the style of dress worn by Princess Marina in 1934 and the dress of her mother, Princess Hélène of Greece, daughter of Prince Vladimir of Russia, when she married in 1902. The differences are not merely reflections of changing styles of dress. Following the tradition established in the nineteenth century, Hélène wore full Russian court dress with a velvet and ermine-trimmed mantle. By contrast, Marina dressed in the latest style by Molyneux. Her taste was described by *The Lady*, in November 1934, as 'perfect'.

On 27 February 1919, only three months after the signing of the Armistice, Princess Victoria Patricia Helena Elizabeth, second daughter of the Duke of Connaught, was married to Commander the Honourable Alexander Robert Ramsay, RN, younger son of the Earl of Dalhousie. The war cast a distinct shadow over the display at the wedding and affected directly both the ceremonial and the dress. It was, in fact, a relatively simple affair and the *Daily Sketch* ran a headline that epitomized popular attitudes: PRINCESS PATRICIA — A SAILOR'S BRIDE. There was to be no carriage procession to Westminster Abbey, where the ceremony took place.

OPPOSITE PAGE: *Lady Elizabeth Bowes-Lyon, who married the Duke of York on 26 April 1923. Her veil was of antique lace lent by Queen Mary, and her bouquet was by Edward Goodyear. (Hulton-Deutsch)*

THIS PAGE, BELOW: *Putting the finishing touches to the wedding cake for the marriage of Princess Mary and Viscount Lascelles. (Hulton-Deutsch)*

The bride, accompanied by her father, left St James's not in a State landau, but in a simpler carriage drawn by four greys. The postillions were wearing what was known as scarlet, not State, liveries. Similarly, the guard of honour were in service, not full dress, in tribute to the recent conflict which had been recalled at a service in the abbey only a few days before the wedding.

The groom wore the simple reefer jacket of a commander in the Royal Navy. Both Princess Patricia's father and grandfather were in field marshal's uniform but, significantly, not in full but service dress order. The khaki tunic, breeches and field boots, worn with brown leather Sam Browne belt blended in well with the dress of other male guests and clearly fulfilled the wishes of the people.

The bride's dress was by Reville and Rossiter. She wore an underdress of silver lace, over which white *broche panne* was caught in lover's knots. The sleeves were long white chiffon and the bodice was draped across the breast and caught by a sash or girdle of silver embroidery which hung in long ends at the left side. This sash was finished in lover's knots and acorns, and there was a bouquet of white heather and myrtle tucked into the front. The train which *The Lady* described as 'full-court length', was of silver cloth embroidered in a design of lilies with a 'great sheaf of monster lilies' in silver at the end. Along the border were large laurel leaves and more silver lilies, all sprinkled with diamonds.

The Lady felt, however, that the glory of the ensemble was the veil. This was of lace as traditional for a royal bride. It was a gift from Lady Sybil Rhonda and was reputedly the same lace worn by Queen Charlotte for her marriage to George III in 1761. It was embroidered with a crown and the cipher *C* within the heart of a rose.

The train was carried by two pages, establishing a new tradition. The Earl of McDuff and the Honourable Simon Ramsay, were wearing their respective tartans; Lady Jean Ramsay, Princess Ingrid of Sweden, Lady Ida Ramsay, Lady May Cambridge, Princess Maud, Princess Mary and the ladies Helen and Victoria Cambridge were the bridesmaids. The elder ladies wore picture hats, another innovative feature of the wedding. Trimmed with wreaths of wild roses, blackberries and foliage, the roses in

green and blue tissue, the hats were of chiffon, in a shade of blue called 'love in a mist'. Their chiffon dresses were a lighter shade of blue and had full skirts falling in pleats from the waist. The bodices were draped over a vest of lace which was embroidered in silver and held at the waist by a deep folded belt of blue, surrounded by folds of rose-pink and green which were designed in bunches of wild roses and leaves. The younger bridesmaids wore simpler dresses in the same shades, but no hats. All carried bouquets of anemones tied with blue gauze.

After the years of war, the pastoral image which the dresses conjured up was no doubt a deliberate reminder of the gentler ways of peace, and of the English countryside. In the bride's dress, too, there were signs and symbols of well-established tradition. The lover's knot, for example, the classical symbol of union, derives from images of Cupid tying a knot between Venus and Mars. The lily, attribute of the Virgin Mary, is a symbol of purity; while laurel, which was represented on the border of the train, is both a symbol of victory and one of everlasting virtues.

Unlike many previous princes and princesses, Patricia did not have the option to choose a spouse from one of the Protestant German Houses, which frequently had provided candidates in the past.

Britain had been at war with Germany and Austria for four years. The King had changed the name of the Royal House from Saxe-Coburg to Windsor; any close connection, so soon after the cessation of

hostilities with the enemy, would have been imprudent, to say the least.

Princess Patricia paid one penalty for her choice of spouse – she relinquished her royal title and emerged from the abbey no longer a princess. It was under the appellation of Lady Ramsay that she drove away from St James's Palace after the reception, wearing a dress of heavy blue silk stockinette, embroidered at the neck and hem, with a cloth belt knotted loosely at the hip. She was applauded by the *Illustrated London News* who called Mrs Handley-Seymour's creation 'the newest design'. The final 'going-away' photograph of the bride and groom, published in contemporary newspapers, showed her leaving in her fashionable dress by motor car, herald of the new age, flanked by her father and grandfather in their khaki service dress. This image was summed up in the message of the Archbishop of Canterbury: 'we find the whole earth at a grand junction between war and peace'.

The influence of war was, however, far from over, as indicated by the royal weddings of 1922 and 1923.

OPPOSITE PAGE: *Prince George, Duke of Kent, and his bride, Princess Marina. Her dress was designed by Molyneux and her bouquet included the traditional sprig of myrtle. (Reproduced by gracious permission of Her Majesty The Queen)*

THIS PAGE, LEFT: *An engagement photograph of the Duke of York (afterwards George VI) and Lady Elizabeth Bowes-Lyon. (Popperfoto).* BELOW: *Princess Patricia, daughter of Prince Arthur, Duke of Connaught, with her husband, the Honourable Alexander Ramsay, after their wedding on 27 February 1919. (Hulton-Deutsch)*

ON her way to marry Henry Viscount Lascelles on 28 February 1922, Princess Mary, daughter of George V, stopped her carriage by the newly erected Cenotaph. At this national memorial to the casualties of war, Regimental Sergeant Major Barwick of the Grenadier Guards placed flowers in remembrance of the fallen. Three years after the signing of the Armistice, the war continued to exert its influence on the everyday lives of the public and the monarchy alike.

The *Illustrated London News* conjured up other images to remind its readers of the service that the couple had rendered during the war: there was a picture of the Princess in her VAD uniform, nursing sick children. In their description of the groom, too, the papers stressed his link with the war. He had served with the Third Battalion of the Grenadier Guards and been awarded the Distinguished

Service Order and the *Croix de Guerre*. Lascelles was described as the 'personification of all things English'.

For his wedding however, he felt it permissible to wear not service but the full dress of the Grenadier Guards. It consisted of a bearskin headdress with white goat's hair plume; a scarlet tunic with blue collar and cuffs, the buttons with the regimental pattern of the Royal Cipher reversed and interlaced, surmounted by a crown, with a grenade beneath the cipher in the centre; overalls of blue cloth with scarlet stripes down the sides, and black boots. The sword had a steel hilt with the regimental device pierced and chased on the guard. It was clearly not the working – or fighting – dress of the contemporary soldier. Its style reflected the middle years of the nineteenth century, rather than the early years of the twentieth. This image of traditional service was repeated by the King who wore the full dress of a

ABOVE: *The marriage of Princess Mary and Viscount Lascelles. The King stands by his daughter's side. Painting by Frank Salisbury. (Reproduced by gracious permission of Her Majesty The Queen)*
OPPOSITE PAGE, TOP RIGHT: *Some of the intense preparations undertaken for a royal wedding. Here, decorative plaques of Princess Mary and Viscount Lascelles are being made. (Hulton-Deutsch).*

colonel of the Grenadier Guards, a gesture to his future son-in-law.

Khaki was not forgotten amidst the scarlet splendours of full dress. A part of the Guard of Honour in Westminster Abbey was formed by the Yorkshire Hussars, who wore service dress and their war medals.

Princess Mary was the first daughter of a monarch to be married in the abbey for centuries. She arrived with her father in the Irish State Coach, a little behind the carriage which had delivered Queen Mary and Queen Alexandra at three minutes past eleven o'clock.

On either side of the sacrium, gold and crimson upholstered chairs had been set out for the royal family and on the altar steps were two kneeling cushions, recently embroidered in Peterborough. One bore the arms of Westminster Abbey and the other, on a gold background, surrounded by a Tudor rose and thistles, the letter *M* for Mary. There were no flowers. The King and Queen had reputedly viewed the abbey, with its display of plate, and decided that floral arrangements were unnecessary. To the splendour of the ecclesiastical plate there were added the scarlet coats, and gilt helmets with white plumes, of the Gentlemen at Arms who, by custom, did not remove their head-dresses inside the abbey.

Amidst this display of traditional uniform and gold plate, the dress of the bride created a fashionable contrast. Princess Mary had made it clear that

A commemorative mug issued to mark the wedding of Princess Mary and Viscount Lascelles, a reminder that the popularity of royal commemoratives is not a recent phenomenon. (Museum of London)

she would have her dress made from materials drawn as far as possible from the Empire. This provided for the Princess a greater market than earlier generations had enjoyed. Her trousseau, however, did follow her mother's precept that all the silk should come from England, all the flannel from Wales, all the tweed from Scotland, and all the linen and poplin from Ireland.

The wedding dress itself was to be white and silver. The underdress, handwoven in cloth of silver, was cut square at the neck and edged with silver lace. Over it was worn a transparent dress of white *marquisette* with a U-shaped neckline, edged in silver and embroidered with pearls, silver and crystal in a raised design of roses and leaves. It hung straight from the shoulders, where it was caught in a cluster of diamonds, falling almost to the ground. Around the low waist was a girdle of twisted silver cloth studded with pearls, finished at the side with a trail of artificial orange blossom. The sleeves were wide and hemmed with pearls; beneath them were tighter sleeves which came to the elbow. Honiton lace lent by Queen Mary had been made into a collar at the back of the dress and it ran down each side to the hem and the edges of the court train.

The train was described by *The Lady* as a 'veritable work of art'. The material had been woven at

Braintree Mills, the warp all white silk – 20,000 threads wide – and every second thread of the weft was silver. It was four yards long and was suspended, as were most court trains at that time, from the shoulder. Upon it were worked emblems of the Empire. There were roses for England, shamrock for Ireland, thistles for Scotland, daffodils for Wales, a maple leaf for Canada and fern leaf for New Zealand. The border continued the Imperial theme with Indian silver lotus flowers. The veil was thrown back over a wreath of orange blossom.

The tiara consisted of three strands of silver over which the orange blossom was arranged, with larger blossoms in the centre and buds resting on the hair. Princess Mary did not carry a bouquet, but instead an illuminated and leather-bound book of the marriage service which her mother had had specially made for her daughter. Her outfit was completed by court shoes of silver brocade, made by ex-servicemen and women. The buckle had a trefoil pattern, the bow in seed pearls on silver tissue. Her gloves of soft, white kid reached almost to the shoulder and she carried a handkerchief edged with Buckingham lace and embroidered with a coronet and the initial *M*.

Her bridesmaids, selected from her many young relatives, wore gowns of ivory satin and silver lace, trimmed with crystal and pearls with a floral design. There was a wide, straight, cloth-of-silver panel

Detail of the train worn by Princess Mary for her marriage to Viscount Lascelles. Described by The Lady *as a 'work of art', it included roses, symbolic of England, in its design. (Earl of Harewood)*

which formed the back and front of the dress, and a sash worn low at the waist was embellished with mother-of-pearl and caught at the side in a large silver rose with a bow of blue velvet. The headdresses were of plaited silver leaves with diamond berries and the bouquets of pale pink sweet peas bound with silver ribbon. They all wore diamond and sapphire brooches engraved with the initials *M* and *H* for Mary and Henry, bride and groom.

The symbolism, rife upon the dress, extended to the wedding cake, although here the references were more personal and less imperial. Made by McVitie and Price the magnificent creation was

BELOW: *The marriage of Princess Mary, eldest daughter of George V, and Viscount Lascelles. Lady Elizabeth Bowes-Lyon was one of the bridesmaids and can be seen second from the left, at the back. (Reproduced by gracious permission of Her Majesty The Queen)*

Lady Elizabeth Bowes-Lyon, daughter of the Earl of Strathmore, on her way to her marriage with the Duke of York in 1923. (Popperfoto)

tained a bouquet of real sweet peas, lilies-of-the-valley, white- and mauve-tipped orchids, roses, and asparagus fern.

Details of dress and cake were reported in the newspapers. On the day itself there were crowds fifteen-deep along the line of the procession to the abbey. It was, according to *The Times*, 'an amazingly big crowd and an amazingly good-humoured one', who watched the carriages, with their escort of the Life Guards, 'the sun shining on their breast plates'; the flowers placed at the Cenotaph; the coster monger who appeared in his Pearly costume by the monument. The cheers of the crowds were heard at Buckingham Palace and answered in Piccadilly. At the palace the royal guests in the State Dining Room sat down to a wedding breakfast which included: *Côtelette d'agneau à la Princess, Chaufroid de poulard à la Harewood*, and *Timbales de Gaufres à la Windsor*.

Following the breakfast, Princess Mary, in a travelling dress of hyacinth blue, her husband beside her in a dark suit, grey overcoat and black silk top hat, left for their honeymoon in Weston Park, Shropshire. Meanwhile, reported *The Times*, the question on everyone's lips was, 'when and whose – will be the next royal marriage at Westminster Abbey?'

I T was the wedding of a future king that next graced the altar of Westminster Abbey, although in 1923 the Duke of York was not heir to the throne. On 26 April 1923 he married Lady Elizabeth Bowes-Lyon, daughter of the Earl of Strathmore. Following the abdication of his eldest brother, the Prince of Wales, the marriage assumed a greater significance.

The groom's clothing indicated links with earlier weddings, although the Duke of York chose to wear the uniform of the Royal Air Force, with whom he had trained at Cranwell. Other royal principals wore the full dress of various services. The King was in his uniform as Admiral of the Fleet, the Prince of Wales wore the full-dress uniform of the Grenadier Guards, while Prince Henry of Gloucester chose naval uniform and Prince George of Kent naval cadet's dress. Uniforms were also worn by many of the guests. This was the

four-tiered and weighed 400 pounds. The first tier was decorated for the Princess. It featured the crests of the Girl Guides, of which she was President, and the Royal Scots, of which she was Colonel-in-Chief. The tier for Viscount Lascelles bore representations of the colours of the Grenadier Guards and the Yorkshire Hussars. Above this, a tier with the couple's respective coats of arms represented their union and, finally, at the top came a tier replete with symbols of love and peace. Cupids were depicted amongst flowers; a silver rose bowl con-

period when court uniforms were still the regulation dress for those attending court and the wedding was, of course, a court occasion. Members of the government and higher civil service wore dark blue coats embroidered with gold. They were distinguished from the similar uniforms of the members of the royal household by the dark blue-black collar and cuffs replacing the household's scarlet facings. Lord Asquith, former Prime Minister, was resplendent in the full dress of an Elder of the Brethren of Trinity House. This was an essentially Royal Navy pattern, but with the addition of scarlet collar and cuffs, and the Trinity House Coat of Arms on the gold bullion epaulettes. The various foreign ministers and ambassadors would wear the dress uniforms of their own countries, and the abbey glittered with gold lace and embroidery hand-worked in uniforms which reflected early nineteenth-century military styles.

Female guests wore fashionable long gowns: the bride's mother, the Countess of Strathmore, was in black *marocain* and georgette with jet and blue paillettes; Lady Elizabeth's sister, Lady Elphinstone, wore a gown of fawn Byzantine satin, embroidered in jade green and trimmed with lace, made by Mrs Handley-Seymour.

At twenty-one, the bride was five years younger than the Duke of York and her dress was described in the pages of *The Times* as, 'the simplest ever made for a royal wedding'. It was of chiffon moire which had been specially dyed to match the colour of the *point de Flanders* lace veil, which had been lent by

Queen Mary. The dress had a deep, square neckline with a narrow piped edge. The sleeves were similarly trimmed. The bodice was cut straight to the waist, with no darts, and the back extended to a separate train. At the front, the skirt was gently pleated into the waist seam. Down the front of the dress was an appliquéd bar of silver lamé with horizontal bars arranged over the bodice to form the appearance of a stomacher; each bar was decorated and edged with gold embroidery and pearl and paste beads. The train at the back, integral to the dress, extended some ten inches beyond the hem and spread eighty-inches wide. Over this was worn the train of antique lace lent by Queen Mary. The veil, of similar lace, was secured by a simple wreath of orange blossom.

Lady Elizabeth's bouquet, created by Edward Goodyear, included roses and lilies-of-the-valley, with a white rose, the emblem of the County of York, at either side. The shoes were of ivory silk moire, made as sandals and embroidered with silver roses. There were eight bridesmaids, all wearing simple dresses. The underdresses of *crêpe de chine* with bands of Nottingham lace were covered with white chiffon. They had elbow-length sleeves. At the waist were silver and white roses fastening sashes of silver lamé and leaf-green tulle. The hair of each bridesmaid was dressed with a narrow fillet of myrtle leaves, white roses, and sprigs of heather.

So dressed, Lady Elizabeth made her way with her attendants into the abbey, stopping to pay homage at the tomb of the Unknown Warrior. If this gesture looked back four years to the war, in the technology that reported the event there were glimmers of the shape of things to come. In addition to the coverage in newspapers and magazines, for the first time films were made of the ceremony and the movements of the newly weds until they made their appearance on the balcony at Buckingham Palace. The films were available for viewing on the very evening of the wedding day. At least twenty-five photographers were employed by Topical Budget to make their film, while the Pathe Gazette made a special feature of the homelife of the Duke and Duchess. Gaumont Graphic used the wedding to test their automatic developing and printing plant. Copying at a rate of thirty prints per hour, the

Detail of the embroidery on the bodice of the wedding dress worn by Elizabeth Bowes-Lyon for her marriage to the Duke of York in 1923. This detail, a portion of the silver lamé appliquéd bar, was decorated and edged with gold embroidery, and pearl and paste beads. (HM Queen Elizabeth, The Queen Mother)

LEFT: *A going-away picture of the Duke of York and his new Duchess, following their wedding in 1923. (Popperfoto).* BELOW: *The wedding cake made by Huntley and Palmers. (Hulton-Deutsch).* BOTTOM RIGHT: *The marriage of the Duke of York to Lady Elizabeth Bowes-Lyon. (National Portrait Gallery)*

company boasted that by nine o'clock on the night of the wedding it had produced twenty-five million feet of film.

ELEVEN years after the wedding of Lady Elizabeth and the Duke of York, Princess Marina, married in 1934 to Prince George of Kent, became perhaps the first royal bride to assume the role of fashion icon, and to have her wedding broadcast on the radio.

Princess Marina was born on 13 December 1906. Because of the turbulence which rocked European monarchies during the early decades of the century, she spent a great deal of her early life travelling from country to country in straightened economic circumstances, making frequent trips to Britain. It was on one of these journeys, in September 1933, that she met the youngest son of George V and Queen Mary. Prince George had served with the Royal

Navy and also spent time working in the Home Office and the Foreign and Diplomatic Service. From very early in their relationship there was media speculation about a possible engagement.

In fact, the media coverage enjoyed by the couple is comparable to the recent experiences of the Prince and Princess of Wales and the Duke and Duchess of York in the 1980s. Perhaps the reasons for this were not entirely a matter of coincidence. A new generation of photogenic royals were in the public eye and the newspapers and other media were keen for the story of a royal romance. Princess Marina and Prince George were attractive, stylish and popular. After news of the engagement had leaked out, the *Daily Express* reported that the country had given Princess Marina a 'burst of welcome as had not been seen since the day Queen Alexandra came across the sea from Denmark seventy-two years ago'.

Marina was, by any standards, an exceptionally beautiful woman, and she complemented her classical good looks with fashionable clothes. Her taste ran to simple lines, allied with the use of the best available fabrics. Her attention to detail – which had her sending back dresses that her eye told her exhibited crooked seams or hems – cast her as the prototype of the royal model, a role now filled by the present Princess of Wales. At the time, *The Lady*

informed its readers that 'England is lucky indeed to acquire a new Princess whose taste in clothes is so perfect'. The magazine advised that sensible people would not slavishly copy Marina's clothes, but instead pay careful attention to the principles that underlied them. These were summed up as, 'plain things, plain, plain, plain'. 'Marina blue', a shade favoured by the Princess, and the small pill-box hats she wore, soon became important elements in the wardrobes of any fashionable woman.

There were certain conditions attached to the design and manufacture of a royal wedding dress that affected the choice of designer. Among others the Princess had been dressed by Jean Patou, acquiring items from the couturier at a discount. Prince George insisted, however, that a British house be chosen for the wedding commission. Fortunately Captain Molyneux, whose taste in the simple line and perfect cut accorded with that of the Princess, had premises in both London and Paris.

Although the design was decided upon well in advance of the wedding, the dress itself was made only two weeks before the ceremony. The silver brocade was made in Lyons and imported at the last moment, but it was nevertheless commended by *The Lady* as a 'gorgeous fabric'. It was woven with a design of Old English roses. The dress was close-fitting with a high neckline, in a style termed

RIGHT: *A group photograph of the wedding of the Duke and Duchess of Kent, 29 November 1934. Marina's simple, but elegant style of dress was copied around the world. (Reproduced by gracious permission of Her Majesty The Queen)*

LEFT: *An official engagement photograph of Princess Marina. Her acclaimed beauty is evident. (Popperfoto).* BELOW: *A hoarding illustrating the popularity of Prince George and Princess Marina. (Hulton-Deutsch)*

'mediaeval' by contemporary commentators; the sleeves fell long and loose. It was a style that later influenced a line of fashionable wedding dresses. From the shoulders hung the court train which was four-and-a-half yards long and lined with silver lamé. The veil was worn off the face, as tradition demanded, and was of old family lace, supplemented by yards of white tulle, and falling to the floor from a diamond tiara. Marina carried a bouquet of lilies, carnations and orchids, which had been grown at Windsor, and as tradition demanded, it included the sprig of myrtle taken from a bush which had grown from a sprig from the bouquet of Princess Victoria, the Princess Royal. Marina wore plain, silver lamé, sandal-style shoes, which fastened around the ankle with a diamond button.

Her six older bridesmaids each wore fine crêpe dresses, woven with silver thread. The lines were less severe than those of the bride, and the bodice took the form of a soft cowl, the skirt flaring from the hips. The two younger bridesmaids, Princess Elizabeth, elder daughter of the Duke and Duchess of York, and Lady May Cambridge, were dressed in frocks of stiff white tulle over silver lamé under-dresses, the high neckline trimmed with a rose design. All wore headdresses of white York roses, which were present in their bouquets tied with silver ribbon.

Molyneux was responsible for much of the trousseau. For day wear, he included slim, narrow-skirted dresses to be worn with loose-fitting jackets, emphasizing the shoulders with such devices as flared epaulettes.

The wedding of Prince George and Princess Marina was broadcast by what the Archbishop of Canterbury called, 'a new and marvellous invention of science'. Radio microphones were placed around the abbey and a commentary was provided before and after the service by Howard Marshall of the BBC – the actual service was deemed too sacred to allow a commentary.

After the ceremony in Westminster Abbey there was another, private, service in Buckingham Palace, according to the rites of the Greek Orthodox

Church, of which Princess Marina was a member. Now the splendidly attired figure of Archbishop Thyateira, in full episcopal habit and carrying his metal-snaked headstaff of office, took the place of the Archbishop of Canterbury. Prince George and Princess Marina were adorned with crowns of blessings and they drank from a communal cup, a symbol of their decision to share their future life together. There were echoes of the marriages of Prince Constantine of Greece and Princess Sophie of Prussia in 1889, as well as Prince Alfred, Duke of Edinburgh, and Grand Duchess Marie in 1874.

THE final royal wedding to be celebrated in the reign of George V was the marriage of Prince Henry of Gloucester and Lady Alice Montagu-Douglas-Scott, daughter of the Duke of Buccleuch, which was celebrated on 6 November 1935.

The Lady made a comment about this wedding that could be deemed the epitome of all royal weddings, certainly those since 1919. 'The public,' wrote the magazine, 'is enthusiastic about magnificent royal functions because they are celebrations of ideal family life, not for their splendour in itself or as an international gesture of dignity and power'. This was indeed a world away from the Hanoverian court – but the world had moved on, and where other European monarchies had declined and fallen, failing to adapt to change, the British royal family was firmly in place at the heart of the Empire.

Perhaps the most interesting aspect of the wed-

ding of the Duke of Gloucester – which was sadly overshadowed by the death of the bride's father – was the choice of Norman Hartnell as designer for the wedding dress. In 1935 he was newly established at 26, Bruton Street, in London's West End. Learning of the engagement of the Duke of Gloucester to Lady Alice, he wrote to the prospective bride to ask if he might be allowed to provide sketches for the wedding dress. In his autobiography, *Silver and Gold*, Hartnell wrote that his letter to Lady Alice and her reply proved the turning-point in his career. Not only was he to design the bride's dress, but also those of the bridesmaids, amongst whom was the Princess Elizabeth, whose own wedding dress he would design a dozen years later.

Lady Alice wore a dress of pale pink satin, with a veil of white tulle. The bouquet was of simple white flowers.

The elder bridesmaids wore dresses of the same fabric as Lady Alice, the younger ones were dressed in short tulle and satin frocks. The ceremony, in respect for the recent death of the Duke of Buccleuch, took place in the private chapel at Buckingham Palace. The couple later appeared on the balcony, when the crowd could see that the relative simplicity of the bride's dress contrasted greatly with the rich colour and splendour of the groom's full-dress uniform of the Tenth Hussars. In this were mixed elements of Eastern European folk dress and Victorian costume. An ostrich feather, inspired by one worn by the Hungarian Cavalry, was set in the headdress, with a black and white feather base. The tunic, essentially a Victorian inspiration, was of blue cloth, edged all around with gold gimp. On each side of the breast were loops of the same gold cord, with caps and drops fastened by gold-worked olivets. The collar and cuffs were edged with gold embroidery and down each side of the blue-cloth overalls were broad stripes of yellow cloth. Over one shoulder was a belt of black patent leather with metal chain ornaments which carried on the back a pouch, also of black patent leather. Even the boots were ornamented with a gold boss, two-inches long and one-and-a-half inches wide.

There was a romantic, almost Ruritanian aspect to this costume – a far cry from the modern world of war. The fossilization of full-dress military uni-

ABOVE: *The Duke and Duchess of Windsor on their wedding day in 1936. The Duchess's dress was by Mainbocher. They forfeited King George's throne for a life of near-exile. (National Portrait Gallery)*

forms is a function of their purpose to epitomize tradition, regimental history and the glory of service to the monarch, having nothing to do with the ephemeral world of fashion. After their appearance on the balcony, the couple drove from Buckingham Palace on the first leg of their journey to Boughton House, in Northamptonshire, for the honeymoon. The Duchess's going-away outfit, like her wedding dress, was by Hartnell and consisted of a dress of misty-grey velvet with a shirred neckline, and sleeves edged with pale-grey fox. A corsage of violets was attached to the waist.

Afterwards, *The Lady* wrote, 'The marriage had given great satisfaction to all classes', perhaps best summing up the spirit of comradeship and national unity inspired by the interwar marriages.

One year later, Edward, the eldest son of George V, married Mrs Wallis Simpson of Baltimore, a divorcee. The wedding took place quietly at the Château de Condé. The bride wore a long, flowing dress of pale blue crêpe satin by Mainbocher, and a hat trimmed with a halo of feathers. The groom wore a simple black morning suit. This marriage cost the Prince of Wales, who had succeeded his father as Edward VIII, the throne. Some called it the end of an era; perhaps it was.

Detail of the beaded embroidery on Princess Elizabeth's wedding dress. There were more than 10,000 pearls in the beautiful embroidered roses, wheat and various flowers that adorned the dress. (Reproduced by gracious permission of Her Majesty The Queen)

and then in some British papers. The dress was still, however, a triumph. It was a one-piece Princess style with a fitted bodice, the neckline having a deep-scalloped edge. The front bodice was cut in three panels, with additional waist and bust darts, and the back was cut in four, fastening down the centre back with buttons and loops. The wrist-length, tight-fitting sleeves ended in embroidered cuffs. From the low-pointed waist, the skirt – cut on the cross – extended to a deep circular train.

At the shoulder there were three covered loops to attach the full court train. Even after the war Hartnell was clearly still working in the tradition, established years before, of royal wedding dresses that demanded a court train. Princess Elizabeth's train was to be fifteen feet long. The design was conceived and executed by Hartnell, who worked with his head embroideress, Miss Ballard, first laying out fifteen yards of tracing paper on his workroom floor and than marking out the pattern in pencil, balancing the proportions on the design as he drew so there would be no weakness in the overall effect. The white roses were in padded satin, and the corn in diamond and pearl embroidery. Additional flower motifs were inserted and Hartnell's vision of Primavera was built up with orange blossom, syringa and jasmine. His predilection for tulle over lace was expressed in the long veil which was held in place by a diamond tiara. Princess Elizabeth's bouquet, which was briefly misplaced at the palace on the morning of the wedding, was supplied by the Worshipful Company of Gardeners and made by

M. H. Longman. It was composed of white orchids, with a sprig of myrtle taken, as was traditional, from the bush grown from Princess Victoria's bouquet.

With the delivery of the dress to the palace Hartnell's work for the wedding was by no means over. He had been commissioned to design and make the dresses of the bridesmaids as well.

Instead of Botticelli, he looked to the royal collection of pictures by Winterhalter, Tuxen and Hayter, for inspiration. The dresses were of ivory silk tulle with a tightly-fitted bodice, the shoulders swathed with a deep *fichu* of pearl-spotted tulle which, in a reference to the bride's dress, was decorated with a trail of appliqué white-satin syringa. The skirt was embroidered with clusters of this flower. The bridesmaids wore wreaths of miniature wheatsheaves, lilies-of-the-valley and London Pride – made of white satin and silver lamé by Jac Limited of London – and carried bouquets, by Moyses Stevens, of white orchids, lilies-of-the-valley, gardenias, white bouvardia, white roses and nerine. The two pages wore Royal Stuart tartan kilts with frilled white shirts and lace jabots.

In his address, the Archbishop of York made clear his belief that, despite the splendour, it had to be

PRINCESS ELIZABETH'S WEDDING DAY

THE ROYAL COUPLE LEAVING WESTMINSTER ABBEY

remembered that the central reason for the ceremony was the same for all who married, from whatever station in life: 'Notwithstanding the splendour of the service, it is in all essentials the same as it would be for any cottager who might be married in some small country church'. Millions listened to every detail of the ceremony brought to them by what the *Illustrated London News* called, 'the strange intimacy of radio'. The immediacy of radio had the effect of making the royal couple more

accessible, and so set the pattern that was to follow throughout the reign of the Queen.

Contemporary accounts of the wedding return again and again to the theme that it reaffirmed family values. Bagehot had commented that a family on the throne brought the pride of sovereignty to the level of everyday life. By extension, then, the family was also seen to include the family of nations that made up the Commonwealth, and these twin concepts were to be important in the New Elizabethan Age. Masefield's poem tried to capture the mood:

> *To those dear lands still calling Britain home*
> *The Crown is still the link with Britain's past*
> *The consecrated thing that must outlast*
> *Folly and hate and other human foam*

THE marriage of Princess Margaret with Anthony Armstrong-Jones, on 6 May 1960, was, perhaps, a clear product of the times – not least in the choice of groom. He was a photographer, a profession that had hitherto not figured in the occupations of royal husbands. Nevertheless, he was a popular choice, enabling many people to identify with the event. His family, as a widely reported remark insisted, had paid income tax!

The first big royal occasion since the Coronation seven years before, it was to be expected that the processional route should be decorated in an appropriate manner. A particularly attractive addition to the decor were flagpoles from which flew white banners decorated with Tudor roses and the ciphers of the couple. At the road junction of The Mall and Stable Yard Road, from which the bride would emerge on her way to the abbey from Clarence House, there was erected an arch of roses with a span of sixty feet. Under this, in the Glass Coach, escorted by the Household Cavalry and accompanied by her brother-in-law, the Duke of Edinburgh, who was to give her away, Princess Margaret drove to Westminster Abbey.

Princess Margaret's dress was also by Norman Hartnell, but was in great contrast to that made for Princess Elizabeth in 1947. The key note was simplicity, with none of the intricate designs in beading that had characterized the earlier dress. This was the

ABOVE: *The wedding of Princess Margaret and Mr Anthony Armstrong-Jones. The bride and groom are accompanied by their best man and eight bridesmaids. (Popperfoto)*

deliberate choice not only of the designer but also of bride and groom, and it was stunningly effective. As *The Times* remarked, 'It seems as if she moved in a soft white cloud'. This effect was due in part to the thirty yards of fine diaphanous silk which comprised the upper layer of the dress alone. The fitted bodice had a V-neck and the skirt flared out in twelve panels. A deep inverted pleat let into the waist at the centre back allowed the dress to be folded out when the bride sat and then fall back into place so that no unsightly creases would show.

The shape of the skirt was produced by the petticoat, constructed from a total of eight layers of silk net. Additional flounces of stiff net ensured that it stood out each side in the form of a *robe de style*.

Although trained, there was no separate court train. The veil was made by St Cyr of Paris and the flowers included the traditional myrtle.

Princess Margaret's shoes were by Edward Rayne; a court style made of white crêpe, they were faced with white satin with a slender two-and-a-half-inch heel.

As she arrived at the altar, the Princess turned and presented her bouquet to Princess Anne, her chief bridesmaid. The young Princess's dress was also designed by Hartnell and was a copy of one which Princess Margaret had worn as her first evening dress at age seventeen. It had been a favourite of her father's. Of silk organdie, with broderie anglaise interwoven with a pale blue ribbon, the waist was

LEFT: *Wedding procession of Princess Mary and Viscount Lascelles, 1922. Oil painting by Sir John Lavery. (Lord Harewood Collection)*

RIGHT: *Close up of a commerorative tin marking the wedding of the Duke and Duchess of York in 1947. (Robert Opie Collection).* BELOW: *The wedding dress worn by Princess Elizabeth in 1947. (Reproduced by gracious permission of Her Majesty The Queen)*

LEFT: *Detail of the bead embroidery on the wedding dress worn by Lady Elizabeth Bowes-Lyon for her marriage to the Duke of York. (HM Queen Elizabeth, The Queen Mother).* BELOW: *Detail of the bead embroidery on the wedding dress worn by Princess Elizabeth in 1947. (Reproduced by gracious permission of Her Majesty The Queen)*

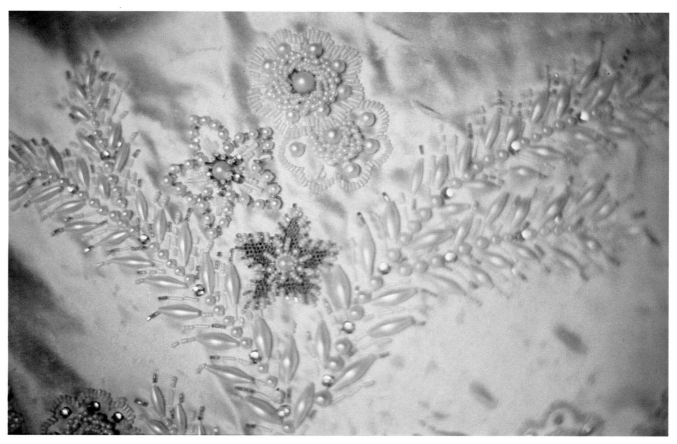

Princess Margaret and
Lord Snowdon with family
and attendants, following
their marriage in 1960.
Photograph by Cecil Beaton.
(Camera Press)

OPPOSITE PAGE: *Princess Anne and Captain Mark Phillips after their marriage in 1973. Photograph by Norman Parkinson. (Camera Press)*

LEFT: *Detail of the beaded underdress worn by Lady Sarah Armstrong-Jones at the wedding of Princess Anne. (HRH The Princess Royal).* BELOW: *Beaded cap worn by Lady Sarah Armstrong-Jones, bridesmaid to Princess Anne in 1973. (HRH The Princess Royal)*

OVERLEAF: *The Prince and Princess of Wales leaving St Paul's Cathedral, after their wedding in 1981. Photograph by Jayne Fincher. (Photographers International)*

Prince Charles looking bemused while Princess Diana waves to the crowds after their wedding. Photograph by J. Applebee. (Alpha)

ABOVE: *The Prince of Wales bows and the Princess curtseys to the Queen, following their marriage, as they leave St Paul's Cathedral. (Syndication International).* RIGHT: *The Prince and Princess of Wales, about to begin their journey back to Buckingham Palace after the wedding. Photograph by J. Applebee. (Alpha)*

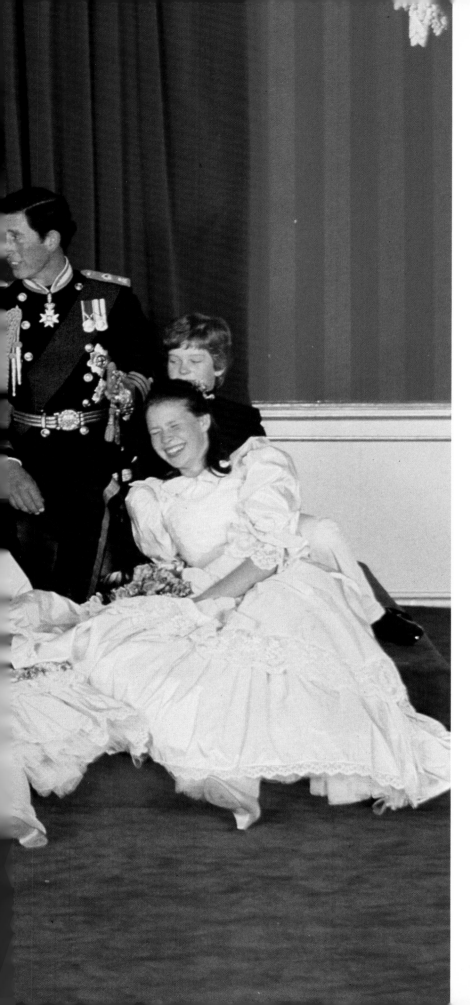

LEFT: *The Prince and
Princess of Wales with their
attendants. Photograph by
Patrick Lichfield. (Camera
Press)*

OVERLEAF: *The Duke and
Duchess of York leaving
Westminster Abbey,
following their marriage in
1986. (Syndication
International)*

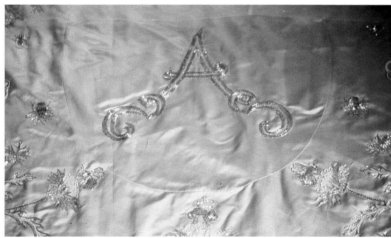

PREVIOUS PAGE, ABOVE:
*The Duke and Duchess of
York returning to
Buckingham Palace.
(Syndication
International).* FAR LEFT,
MIDDLE: *Detail of the end
of the train on The Duchess
of York's wedding dress.
(HRH The Duchess of
York).* FAR LEFT,
BOTTOM: *Embroidered and
beaded bee detail on the
wedding dress of HRH The
Duchess of York. (HRH
The Duchess of York).*
RIGHT: *The anchor motif,
symbolizing Prince
Andrew's naval service,
embroidered on the Duchess
of York's train. (HRH The
Duchess of York)*

RIGHT: *The Duchess of
York alights from a
helicopter in her going-away
outfit. Photograph by Glenn
Harvey. (Syndication
International)*

high and the neck finished in a Peter Pan collar with a grosgrain-ribbon bow. The fullness of the skirt was created by layered petticoats of stiff net. White kid shoes and a small headdress of white ribbon bows and flowers completed the outfit.

The ceremony was seen by literally millions of people, television cameras having been set up throughout the abbey. At Heathrow, recordings of the television pictures were made and despatched by Vulcan bomber to the United States and Canada.

Outside, thousands of people lined the route back to Buckingham Palace – eager for a glimpse of what *The Times* described as a 'Cinderella-like occasion with a dazzling array of golden pageantry'. After the wedding breakfast, at which the band of the Grenadier Guards played, the couple appeared on the balcony before leaving for their honeymoon in the West Indies. For her going-away outfit the Princess chose a coat and dress by Victor Stiebel. The coat was of pale, sunshine yellow in pure silk shantung, cut straight and loose and with a small stand collar and three-quarter-length sleeves. The dress beneath was of fine silk chiffon.

B Y now Westminster Abbey seemed the natural home for royal weddings. The second of the 1960s marriages, however, took place nearly two hundred miles to the north, in York Minster. This was the choice of Lady Katharine Worsley who, in 1962, married the Duke of Kent. The architecture and scale of York Minster, so different from that of Westminster Abbey, was to influence the design of the dress. Furthermore, the construction of the dress had necessarily to accommodate the need for the bride to be able to move freely and undertake the traditional act of obeisance to the Queen without fear of tripping or tearing the dress.

These became the problems of John Cavanagh, the designer chosen by Lady Katharine. He favoured, as Hartnell had for Princess Margaret, a simple line. The dress was made in silk organdie. There was a round boat-neck with a soft, rolled collar and the bodice was darted into the waist. The wrist-length sleeves were tight-fitting and extended over the back of the hand and fastened with twelve

self-covered buttons and loops. There was a waist belt which fastened at the back and had a false bow in the centre. The skirt was very full and lined with silk chiffon, under which there were several net petticoats. The train was attached under the waist belt. Made from the same material as the dress, and lined with two layers of silk chiffon, the train was tightly gathered to the waist but left loose at the hem, giving a sense of lightness as the bride moved. The train was of great length, extending to fifteen feet with a width at the bottom of seventeen feet. The size of train was calculated to complement the lofty dimensions of the Minster.

Lady Katharine was attended by three pages and

BELOW: *The Duke of Kent leaves York Minster with his bride, Lady Katharine Worsley, underneath a guard of honour formed by the swords of his regiment, the Scots Greys. (Popperfoto)*

The false bow fastening the waist-belt of the Duchess of Kent's wedding dress. The dress was designed for Lady Katharine by John Cavanagh, and was made of silk organdie. (HRH The Duchess of Kent)

cess Alexandra were dressed by Cavanagh – Princess Marina in pale, corn-coloured silk organdie embroidered with gold, diamanté and topaz, and Princess Alexandra in coral silk organdie.

With the exception of the groom, few of the men wore uniforms. The Duke of Kent appeared in his magnificent full-dress uniform of the Scots Greys. The tunic was of scarlet wool, with a deep-blue collar and cuffs. The cuffs themselves were ornamented with an embellishment known as an Austrian knot, in round-backed gold cord. The overalls were of dark-blue cloth, with yellow stripes one-and-three-quarter-inches wide down each side. Under the plaited gold shoulder cords, passed the belt of gold lace which held the black leather, silver-trimmed pouch. He also wore the Star and Sash of the Order of the Garter. After early rain, sun shone and *The Times* reported that the bells peeled over a city that was celebrating an essentially Yorkshire wedding. The accents of the crowd were mainly those of county folk – not the transatlantic drawls that would have been heard in London. It reported that the climax of the occasion was the appearance of the Duchess: 'the white cirrus of her veil and the astonishing magnificence of her train' transformed the 'moment into romance' at the first royal wedding in York Minster for 633 years.

eight bridesmaids. The pages wore yellow silk jackets with white collars and knee breeches, and the bridesmaids, the chief of whom was Princess Anne, were in Victorian-style, full-length dresses of white embroidered organdie and caps of white roses.

Apart from the bride and her bridesmaids, none of the ladies wore floor-length dresses. The Queen wore an ensemble that had been originally designed by Hartnell for her recent Italian visit. It consisted of a soft lilac satin dress and coat, with a hat in swathed tulle to match. Princess Marina and Prin-

LESS than two years after the Duke of Kent's wedding, his sister, Princess Alexandra, was married in Westminster Abbey on 24 April 1963, to the Honourable Angus Ogilvy, younger son of the Earl of Airlie.

Unlike Princess Margaret's wedding, this was not to be a State occasion or a public holiday. There was no horse-drawn carriage to take the bride from her home in Kensington Palace, but, instead, the latest addition to the royal fleet of Rolls Royce cars – a maroon vehicle, with a hood that could be pushed back for the admiring crowds to see the bride.

For the Princess John Cavanagh made a dress that was described at the time as supremely traditional in all but the use of colour. The underdress was of white tulle, embroidered with gold paillettes which shimmered as the Princess moved. It had a simple, close-fitting bodice with a high round neck-line and full-length sleeves. The bodice flowed into the skirt in an unbroken line – straight at the front, full and trained at the back. Over this dress was a matching garment in lace, which had been dyed magnolia, and which featured an oakleaf and acorn design. This pattern had been suggested to Cavanagh by the lace worn by Lady Patricia Ramsay when she was married in 1919 – which was reputed to have belonged to Queen Charlotte.

Cavanagh had initially designed a twenty-one-foot train and, with the agreement of the Princess, he suspended this not from the shoulders, but integrated it into the headdress. It fell from the diamond fringe tiara worn earlier by Princess Marina at her wedding in 1934.

The chief bridesmaid was Princess Anne, who looked to *The Times* reporter 'strikingly adult' as she stood alone in the aisle while the couple knelt at the

OPPOSITE PAGE, BOTTOM: Lady Katharine, now the Duchess of Kent, alights from the wedding car, and has her train arranged. (Syndication International)

THIS PAGE, BELOW: *The wedding of Princess Alexandra and the Honourable Angus Ogilvy, 24 April 1963. Princess Marina stands behind the groom and Princess Anne to the left of the bride. (Syndication International)*

altar. Her hair was worn up in a chignon and was encircled by a heavy silk bandeau. All of the bridesmaids wore long dresses in the same shade of magnolia as the bride's lace. They had closely fitting bodices with elbow-length sleeves and plain, round necklines. The gently flared skirts had at the waist a narrow belt with a bow in front.

THE marriage of Prince Michael of Kent and Baroness Marie-Christine von Reibnitz took place at the Town Hall of Vienna on 30 June 1978. With the bride a Roman Catholic – and divorced – a church wedding was not possible without special papal dispensation. This had not been granted. For the compulsory civil ceremony, which was consequently organized, the bride chose to wear an elegant suit of cream silk – hastily made by Hardy Amies. The fitted jacket fastened at the waist with a tie belt and the matching silk blouse was also tied with a bow at the neck. Her hair was fastened back into an ornamental hair-net, decorated with gardenias. The groom wore a pin-striped lounge suit.

The day after this quiet ceremony a private mass was held in the flower-filled Schottenstift Chapel. The Archbishop of Canterbury would also hold a service of blessing for the couple at Lambeth Palace on their return to London.

Prince Henry Duke of Gloucester and his wife Princess Alice had two children. It was the younger son, Richard, who succeeded his father to the dukedom in 1974 following the death of Prince William in an aeroplane accident. On 8 July 1972 Prince Richard married the daughter of a prominent Danish lawyer, Birgitte van Deurs, in the country church at Barnwell, near the family home in Northamptonshire. Although a cousin of the Queen, Prince Richard was a comparatively long way from the throne, according to the Act of Succession, and his wedding was not classed as a major royal event.

The private nature of the ceremony was accentuated by the exclusion of the Press from the church and the fact that there were no bridesmaids or pages. Royal guests included the Queen Mother, in a coat of duck's-egg blue, and Princess Margaret in primrose yellow, both armed against the rain with plastic umbrellas. The Prince of Wales attended in a grey morning suit; Prince Richard also wore morning dress. His bride wore a gown by Hartnell. It was figured silk organdie, with a design of lilies. The front was cut in three straight panels with the shape of the bust defined by darts. The white tulle veil was edged with white organdie piping and held in place by a simple band of stephanotis. Princess Alice, the groom's mother, had made the bouquet, which was based on a traditional Danish design and featured white and cream flowers bound by a satin ribbon.

BELOW: *Princess Alexandra wore a dress by John Cavanagh in which the train fell not from the shoulders but from the diamond tiara. (Syndication International)*

THE trio of royal weddings celebrated during the 1960s have, in retrospect, a great deal in common. The simplicity of the line of the dresses and the use of fabrics – without the heavy symbolic embroideries that had been thought appropriate for the dress of an heir to the throne in 1947 – had given them a unity that accorded with a period when old values were being questioned. Nevertheless, they all included, with the exception of Princess Margaret's dress, the traditional court train.

In reportage, the weddings reflected technological advance – first with radio and then with television, the experience of the event was brought directly into the homes of the people. They also remained great occasions for the spectators who stood in the crowds, for whom radio and television did not give the sense of immediacy and intimacy in sharing a common experience. And, as highlighted by a lady from Newcastle who, when asked why she had not stayed at home to watch the wedding, replied, 'You don't get the colour on TV do you'.

TOP RIGHT: *Prince Richard of Gloucester and his Danish bride, Birgitte van Deurs, were married quietly on a rainy July day in 1972. (Syndication International)*. LEFT: *Princess Alexandra and her chief bridesmaid, Princess Anne, examining a bangle presented to Princess Anne. (Syndication International)*

ROMANTIC
REVIVALS

THE wedding of Princess Anne with Captain Mark Phillips in November 1973 was, in terms of the media coverage of such events, the most sophisticated and widely reported to that date. Colour television pictures, an explosion of souvenirs and the relief – articulated by newspapers and magazines – that such a colourful event could still take place in a country where social disorder and economic decline seemed poised to plumb new depths, seem, in retrospect, the salient features of the occasion.

In view of the prevailing economic difficulties, the royal family wanted the wedding to be a relatively low-key affair. Public appetite, however – and the technology which fed it – demanded a show of traditional royal splendour.

The setting was once again Westminster Abbey, which provided a grand stage for the spectacle. The groom, although a commoner, had a military background and was therefore entitled to wear a colourful full-dress uniform. One important departure from recent tradition was the choice of designer for the wedding dress. In place of Hartnell, or any of the favoured couturiers, Princess Anne placed the commission with one of her favourite designers – Maureen Baker, who worked for Susan Small, in Sloane Street at the time. This led to rumours that the dress would be 'off the peg' and therefore unsuitable for a royal bride. Prudence Glyn, writing in *The Times*, discounted this. She pointed out that although the dress might be unremarkable in design, it was cut to a very high standard. It included many of the Princess's favourite design features, including a high-stand neckline and a tailored bodice.

The dress was of fine, soft satin, lined with plain-weave silk – which had been woven to Maureen Baker's strict instructions at Sudbury in Suffolk, employing a special weave that used more than one thousand threads of twenty denier silk to every inch.

The bodice was closely fitted and the mediaeval-style hanging sleeves were tight to the elbow and then featured a deep, flowing cuff. There was an undersleeve of pleated chiffon ending in a buttoned cuff. At the front the dress was made in four gored panels, with the additional shaping of the waist provided by tucking. The slightly raised collar was edged with pearls and paste, decoration which also appeared on the shoulders. From the waist the skirt flared out. The train, of silk organza, extended five feet from the hem of the dress, and had a pattern of stylized flowers embroidered in floss silk and silver thread with trailing foliage, carried out by S. Lock Limited. Both flowers and foliage were trimmed with pearls and paste. Over this was placed a veil of tulle, supplied by John Heathcoat and Company Limited.

The bridesmaid, Lady Sarah Armstrong-Jones, daughter of Princess Margaret, wore a pinafore dress of stiff white silk over a blouse of fine silk organza, embellished with silk-satin ribbon arranged in a lattice pattern. Each ribbon was given a border of tiny pearls. The long, fitted sleeves fastened at the wrist with press studs. The headdress took the form of a Juliet cap made of fine-weave silk covered with silk organza, the crown covered with a lattice of silk-satin ribbon, echoing the decoration on the bodice. The female members of the royal family in the congregation had no dress regulations to follow and it is interesting to note that the choice of designers fell between the established houses and the newer, younger generation of dressmakers.

OPPOSITE PAGE: *The Prince and Princess of Wales, following their wedding in 1981. (Syndication International)*

BELOW: *Detail of the train worn with the wedding dress of the Princess of Wales. (HRH The Princess of Wales)*

tieth. The full-dress gilt helmet had a black plume, according to the regulations for the Queen's Bays. The scarlet tunic had a collar and cuffs of dark-blue velvet, embroidered with gold lace of regimental pattern and the badge with BAYS on the front. The tunic fastened with eight gilt buttons, on which were embossed the regimental insignia; on the cuffs was sewn an Austrian knot in gold cord. The full-dress overalls in blue cloth had a wide white stripe down each side.

Captain Phillips' sword was put to good use at the wedding breakfast, when it was used to cut the cake which had been made by the Army Catering Corps. The band of the Grenadier Guards played in the background. Following now established tradition, the couple appeared on the balcony of Buckingham Palace before setting off on their honeymoon.

Television companies throughout the world relayed colour coverage of the day. In New Zealand, rental firms reported a sudden rush to obtain sets. In France, an estimated ten million tuned into the coverage of the wedding. It was later estimated that, throughout the world, the wedding was watched by hundreds of millions of people. In Britain – where the government had just declared a state of emergency, considering the current situation in the coal and electricity industries a threat to the essentials of the life of the community – the splendour of the occasion worked its familiar magic, and the newspapers reported that both the fuel crisis and the state of emergency were temporarily forgotten.

For example, the Queen and the Queen Mother were dressed by Hartnell – the Queen in a double-breasted coat of sapphire-blue silk, and the Queen Mother wearing what *The Times* described as a dress and coat of Byzantine splendour, in gold over ivory-beige silk. On the other hand, the younger royal ladies could afford to be more adventurous, combining simple silhouettes with opulent dress fabrics. For the Duchess of Kent, Bellville Sassoon made an outfit in ochre pink and brown velvet, the material recalling the carvings of the Alhambra.

There was, however, nothing fashionable about Captain Phillips' dress. His uniform – made for him by the regimental tailors, Dege and Son, of 16, Clifford Street, in July 1973, only four months before the wedding – was in a style more reminiscent of the nineteenth century than the late twen-

B Y 1981, there had not been a wedding of an heir to the throne for thirty-four years – or the marriage of a Prince of Wales for over a century. This long gap, together with the more accessible image of royalty portrayed, for example, in the 1968 film *The Royal Family*, would have a significant impact on the wedding and indeed the wedding prospects of Prince Charles. It is, therefore, not surprising, that the royal wedding of 29 July 1981, produced an outpouring of comment, analysis and general enthusiasm. The *Daily Express* felt that 'It was as if the whole world had stopped for the wedding'. And at the same time, it was pointed out that the way in which the wedding was conducted

VII, was married to Catherine of Aragon.

In her choice of designers for the wedding dress Lady Diana also broke with tradition, choosing not Hartnell or one of the more established houses, but the Emanuels. Lady Diana had been photographed by Lord Snowdon for *Vogue*, wearing a pink chiffon blouse designed by the Emanuels. It was reputedly this encounter which directed her attention to the designers. They subsequently made the black taffeta, strapless evening gown in which Lady Diana was photographed for her first official engagement, after the marriage had been announced. The dress – with its daring cut – attracted some adverse criticism.

In terms of the historical context of dress worn at court, such comment is curious – unless special dispensation had been obtained from the Lord Chamberlain's Office, dress for court functions had always included a low-cut bodice. In an odd way the views expressed about the dress were a reversal of the more *liberal* Victorian values. Nevertheless, the black dress was not seen again in public. The Princess's wardrobe and her wedding dress undoubtedly influenced fashion and, as David Emanuel said, he believed Lady Diana saved the tradition of dressing up.

There was great secrecy surrounding the design and manufacture of the wedding dress. No sketches were drawn, and blinds were kept firmly down in the workroom. Speculation that the dress would feature an off-the-shoulder style was to prove incorrect and, although the complexity of the design would, felt David Emanuel, tax the copyist, the first replica was in the windows of Debenham's depart-

showed how the monarchy 'has smoothly adapted to the changing needs of our times infinitely better than so many of our institutions'.

In many ways, however, the organization of the wedding – and the dress worn to it – was steeped in tradition. Although one Labour MP had, before the event, expressed the wish that the couple would wear blue jeans and thereby boost the British manufacture of denims, David and Elizabeth Emanuel, who designed the wedding dress, wanted to transform Lady Diana Spencer into 'A fairytale princess', reflecting both the personality and image of the 'young and lively bride'. This choice of dress would better accord with the traditional expectations of the people, just as Prince Charles's naval uniform would present a more traditional picture of royalty.

There was one clear break with twentieth-century practice. Prince Charles decided to be married in St Paul's Cathedral, rather than Westminster Abbey. This was prompted by his passion for the cathedral's architecture and by the practical consideration that it would seat more people than the abbey. It recalled, too, the fact that over five hundred years previously, in old St Paul's, another Prince of Wales, Arthur, son of Henry

Detail showing the stylized embroidery on the train of Princess Anne's dress. The train itself was of silk organza, and the embroidery was carried out by S. Lock Limited. (HRH The Princess Royal)

ment store only five hours after the service in St Paul's. In polyester satin, it was priced at £450.

Jean Rook, writing in the *Daily Express*, described the bride as 'one great creamery ivory thrill'. The original dress was of ivory-coloured silk taffeta. The bodice was fitted and boned with a deep flounce around the gently curving neckline. It featured Carrickmacross lace panels on both front and back, embroidered with mother-of-pearl sequins and pearls. The full sleeves were gathered and trimmed with an elaborately embroidered lace flounce. The skirt was given its fullness by a crinoline petticoat, which was composed of many layers of ivory tulle over stout nylon net. In order to incorporate an element of blue – there is a popular ideology which claims that a bride wearing some blue is brought good fortune – a small blue bow was sewn into the waistband. A small eighteen-carat gold horseshoe, made by Douglas Buchanan, was also stitched into the waist.

The train, of the same taffeta, was twenty feet long and hung from the waist. It was not, however, specifically referred to as a court train. Designers were no longer working in the established conventions of court dress which had been part of the vocabulary of royal wedding dresses as late as the 1960s.

Lady Diana's veil of ivory silk tulle, which glinted with hand-embroidered mother-of-pearl sequins, fell from a diamond tiara – part of the Spencer family collection. Diamond earrings, lent to the bride by her mother, completed Lady Diana's jewellery. Diana's shoes were by Clive Shilton, made of ivory silk and embroidered with a diamond pattern. In the centre of each diamond, a mother-of-pearl sequin was sewn, and over each vamp was a heart-shaped rosette, embroidered with gold beads and sequins, and edged with lace. Each shoe had a slightly pointed toe and even the soles were painted with a design of stylized flowers.

The wedding bouquet – a gift from the Worshipful Company of Gardeners – was made, as had all royal wedding bouquets since the war, with the exception of Princess Anne's, by Longmans. Together with his senior florist, Doris Welham, David Longman made Lady Diana's bouquet after de-

BELOW: *The wedding of the Prince and Princess of Wales. Inside St Paul's Cathedral. (Syndication International)*

tailed discussions with the bride and her dress designers. Despite the fact that the exact design of the dress could not be revealed, Longman garnered sufficient information to enable him to create a bouquet which would complement it. Spares were prepared for emergencies; the memory of the mislaid bouquet on Queen Elizabeth's wedding day was fresh enough to ensure no chances were taken.

In the centre of the bouquet were gardenias, supported, in memory of Lord Mountbatten, by the roses that bear his name. A cascade of white odontoglossom orchids complemented the centrepiece. From this fell a shower of stephanotis, supported by miniature tradescantia leaves. As tradition demanded, myrtle completed the bouquet.

Lady Diana was supported by five bridesmaids, the chief of whom was Lady Sarah Armstrong-Jones. All wore dresses based on the design of the bride's dress, but in a lighter-weight silk. Lady Sarah's dress was full length and the bodice was fitted and decorated with beaded lace. The full sleeves were drawn in at the elbow, beautifully embellished by lace flounces. The waist sash was of old gold taffeta and it tied in a bow at the back. The dress had a double skirt, with the overskirt trimmed with beaded lace. The younger bridesmaids wore similar dresses but they hung to mid-calf. All of the shoes were made by Ivory, and were constructed of gold twill silk to match the waist sash. Lady Sarah's shoes were a low-heeled court style, while her little companions wore flat pumps with straps. Lady Sarah carried a loose spray of English-grown garden flowers, with two sprays of the same flowers in her hair. The younger bridesmaids wore flower circlets and carried floral baskets.

The image conjured up by the Emanuels was essentially romantic and indeed fulfilled the hopes that the wedding dress would provide a fairytale element to the event. In a sense, the naval uniform worn by the groom and other male principals was also romantic, far-removed from the practical working dress of sailors. The strong dark blue and gold of the uniform provided an attractive visual contrast to the dresses of the bride and her bridesmaids.

Prince Charles wore the full-dress uniform of a commander in the Royal Navy. The coat was cut

from blue Venetian cloth and had two rows of six buttons down the front. The collar was of white super-fine cloth and edged with gold lace – which was also used on the cuffs, in three bands to denote the Prince's rank. On his right shoulder, as an aide-de-camp to the Queen, Prince Charles wore his gold cord aiguillette. This interesting accoutrement, which terminated in gold points, was derived from a once-practical element in male dress – the cord and points had been used for lacing together the coat. The aiguillette has become a symbol of office – time elevating it to a grander status and transforming the base cord into gold ropes – demonstrating how the fossilization of an element of dress can provide important features of uniform.

On the left-hand side of Prince Charles' chest were pinned the Stars of the Orders of the Garter, Thistle and Bath, and the blue ribbon of the Garter was worn across the chest. At his neck was the Cross of the Grand Master of the Order of the Bath and, above the Stars on his chest, the Coronation and Jubilee Medals.

Also in full-dress uniform, the Duke of Edinburgh wore campaign medals, the Garter and Thistle Stars and the neck-badge of the Order of Merit. Prince Andrew, who acted as supporter for his elder brother, was in naval uniform – Number Five Order, with a reefer jacket and midshipman's sword. At the neck he wore the badge of a

ABOVE: *Lady Diana Spencer's attendants in St Paul's Cathedral, just moments before she became the Princess of Wales. Photograph by R. Slade. (Camera Press)*

Commander of the Royal Victorian Order, and to his chest was pinned the Jubilee Medal.

Apart from Prince Edward – who at the time was not serving in the armed forces – all of the male principals were in service uniform. In the essentially unfashionable nature of this costume, there were, however, proclaimed the virtues of service, loyalty and duty. And despite the revolution in social attitudes that has taken place since the 1960s, it is hard to conceive of a male costume that would adhere more closely to these principles – rather than the whims of style.

The costumes of pages at royal weddings illuminate another feature of dress history. At any wedding, one can see costume used to reflect some element in family history, albeit with overtones of fancy dress. Small boys do not as a rule wear kilts of family tartan, as did the pages at the wedding of Princess Alexandra and the Honourable Angus Ogilvy. Nor do they habitually dress as Victorian sailors.

This was the costume chosen for the pages in 1981. Both wore the full-dress royal naval uniform of 1863, the date of King Edward VII's – then Prince of Wales – marriage. The tail coats were of dark blue cloth, with white cords emblematic of cadet status on the collar; gilt buttons, engraved with the fouled anchor device, adorned the front. The trousers were white – the correct colour for summer wear – and the short dirks, with their gilt hilts and gilt bullion knots, hung directly from the belt in Victorian fashion, rather than from slings as they would today. On the caps were wire-embroidered Victorian royal naval cap badges, scaled down from those worn by officers in 1863.

To relay pictures of the ceremony, twelve camera positions were established by the BBC within the cathedral, and more than sixty cameras were used. Over eighty broadcasting organizations from fifty countries took live pictures from the BBC, thereby ensuring that millions of people were able to watch the ceremony. Souvenir issues of national newspapers included colour pictures of the couple, details of the ceremony, and the route to and from the cathedral.

The sale of commemorative paraphernalia exceeded that of all other royal weddings. Royal wedding souvenirs were first made on a significant scale in 1816, for the marriage of Princess Charlotte, and a number of wares were sold in 1973 for the wedding of Princess Anne. These included a Paragon 'Loving Cup' in a limited edition and a colourful, gilt-embossed Wedgwood mug. For the Prince of Wales' wedding, Staffordshire Potteries had produced an approved design within a day of the announcement of the marriage. They were, in fact, the first of no less than forty-two different firms who produced designs. By the wedding day it was estimated that there were more than 1600 different souvenirs on display. These ranged from a box of matches, which cost three pence, to a canteen of silver cutlery made by Garrard priced at £7500. There was also a Prince of Wales long-case clock, silver dishes, wine labels, caddy spoons, goblets and thimbles – all spilling from the commemorative cornucopia, and many sold with the implication that they would prove worthwhile investments. Some, as the *Evening Standard* remarked, would have been better left on the drawing board – although future historians would have been thus deprived of some interesting source material on the popular image of the monarchy. Some unique – and, perhaps, startling – memorabilia included the reproduction of the couple's picture on a variety of items (including T-shirts), and the production of a Lady Diana car-waver, a royal wedding tea cosy and Prince Charles coat-hanger.

For the first time there was also a wedding video available to the general public. The event would be replayed time and time again in homes throughout

LEFT: *Lady Diana Spencer is led up the aisle of St Paul's Cathedral by her father, Earl Spencer. (Syndication International).* ABOVE: *The Prince and Princess of Wales leaving St Paul's Cathedral after their wedding. The new Princess gazes happily at the crowds. (Camera Press)*

the world, elevating the couple to the status of television stars. The royal wedding of 1981 marks the maturity of the relationship of the media with the royal family. Just as the presence of television has altered our perception of the world and the society in which we live, so it has now altered our image of the royal family.

After the wedding breakfast, and the traditional appearance on the balcony, the couple left for their honeymoon, which began at Broadlands. Perhaps consciously, the Princess of Wales was also embarking on her career as royal fashion model, in a pink silk tussore dress with a matching bolero. The dress had a white collar of silk organza, edged with a frill, and a cummerbund at the waist. According to the *Evening Standard*, this day marked, 'the wedding of the century'.

These superlatives were, however, to be used once again – just five years later when Prince Andrew was married to Miss Sarah Ferguson.

LINKING the weddings of the Prince of Wales and Prince Andrew – and indeed several of the royal weddings recorded in this book – was the design and construction of the ring. Gold, from the mine at Clogau St Davids in Wales, was used for the wedding rings of the Duchess of York in 1923, Princess Elizabeth in 1947, Princess Margaret and Princess Anne, as well as for the Princess of Wales and the Duchess of York, the title which Sarah

Ferguson assumed when she married Prince Andrew in 1986.

There were similarities, too, in the dress worn at the weddings. As at the wedding of the Prince of Wales, there was widespread wearing of uniforms. The dress designed by Lindka Cierach for Miss Ferguson, however, represented in many respects a contrast to that worn by the Princess of Wales. For the first time since 1947, a designer executing a commission for a royal wedding dress used beadwork embroidery on a grand scale. The symbols incorporated in the designs were, however, different. In 1947 Hartnell deliberately chose to invoke through his use of symbols, a better future after the war years – obviously aware of the fact that he was designing a dress for a future Queen. The dress for Miss Ferguson would collate aspects of her own individual taste: there was no need to incorporate national or indeed imperial emblems.

Like the Emanuels, Lindka Cierach had to consider the impact the dress would have on television viewers and she therefore spent some time at Westminster Abbey, where the wedding was to be held and against whose architecture the dress would be set. She needed to produce a design that would make a strong visual statement. The final design would necessarily be the outcome of extensive discussions with the bride. The design of the embroidery was constricted by the availability of beads: the

variety that Hartnell had been able to obtain was simply no longer available. Grand-scale beadwork requires an appropriate ground fabric to support the embroidery, and after an extensive search, it was discovered that English silk would prove unsatisfactory; the fabric was imported from Italy. The lace, however, was all English, designed by Hal Fields and made by Roger Watson in Nottingham.

Ivory silk duchesse satin was used to create the dress. The bodice was fitted and boned and comprised five shaped panels, ending in a low pointed waist at the front. The sleeves, gathered into the shoulder seams, were cut full and ended at the elbow. Like the sleeves, the round neckline was edged with pearl beads. Flat, stylized bows – recalling the shoulder knots of some military uniforms – were arranged on each shoulder and constructed from fine organza, embroidered throughout with beads. The flaring skirt extended at the back into a deep circular train. The underskirt, which helped to achieve this shape, was finished with a scalloped lace flounce.

The front of the bodice was embroidered with a central motif, derived from the Ferguson family crest, of a thistle, attended by three bumble bees, within a border of scrolling ribbons. The sleeves were embroidered with bunches of thistles, tied together with ribbon, and surrounded by bees.

In the tradition of nineteenth-century court trains, Sarah Ferguson's train was fastened at the waist. Seventeen-and-a-half feet long, it flowed from beneath a large bow at the back. The main body was made from three widths of silk satin. It was on the train that the embroidery reached its full expression – the scale increasing as it reached the hem. Based again on the bride's family crest, there were additional anchors and waves, emblematic of Prince Andrew's naval service. All of the beading was composed of iridescent sequins, pearl beads, and silver, gold and transparent bugles. At the bottom of the train, positioned within the deep border, was a cipher entwining the initials A and s. Over the train fell the veil of silk tulle, beaded throughout with sequins. It was given a scalloped border, interspersed with guipure bows.

Designed by Jane Packer, the headdress was trim-

med with heavily scented lily of the valley, clusters of cream roses and gardenias. The tiara, borrowed from a family friend, was composed of a leaf scroll and a diamond collet, mounted in platinum. In addition, Miss Ferguson wore a necklace of cultured pearls, interspersed with roundels of eighteen-carat gold and diamonds, with a lozenge centre in diamond and pearl. A pair of marquise diamond-cluster earrings completed her jewellery. Jane Packer also designed the bouquet, which was presented by the Worshipful Company of Gardeners. A line of ivory gardenias had in the centre cream lilies. To achieve a warm and creamy effect, no foliage (aside from the traditional myrtle) was used.

Miss Ferguson's shoes, by Manolo Blahnik, were of a court style with a blunted-point toe and a low Louis heel – the vamp cut to a shallow point. They were made of satin, covering fine kid, and were lined with gold kid. The satin, which matched the dress, was beaded in a design of bees and ribbons to echo once more the beadwork design of the dress and train. Zara Phillips, one of four bridesmaids, wore a dress of apricot silk faille, with a short-fitted bodice, a square neckline and short, capped sleeves. The V-shaped panel on the front of the bodice was embellished with apricot-coloured lace, woven with a design of thistles, and embroidered with sequins and pearls. At the base of the 'v' was a bow of fine satin ribbon, and a larger bow was positioned at the back. The back of the skirt was cut away to reveal frills of apricot lace.

The bridesmaids' shoes were designed and made by G. S. Glanville Sharp, and covered with the same fabric as the dress. They were decorated with a knot of apricot lace, trimmed with fine satin ribbon. The headdresses took the form of half-circlets of peach roses, lily of the valley and freesias. Hoops bound with satin ribbon and entwined with garlands of flowers to match the headdress were carried by the bridesmaids.

Throughout the wedding day, there was great interest focussed on what other members of the royal family and, in particular the Princess of Wales, were wearing. Princess Diana's dress was designed by Victor Edelstein and made of turquoise and black silk-satin with a polka-dot pattern. The neck-line was 'v'-shaped, with three-quarter-length sleeves. At the waist was a pleated cummerbund, and the skirt fell to the knee. Her hat, in fine straw matching the dress, turned up with a rippled trim. The Queen was dressed by Ian Thomas in a delphinium-blue silk crêpe dress, while Princess Margaret wore a dress designed by Roger Brines, now working at Hartnell. Both the older generation of couturiers and the younger designers were well represented at the wedding.

Male members of the royal family were again in uniform, continuing the tradition established during the closing years of the eighteenth century. Before this time, and the practice of hundreds of years, men dressed as magnificently as ladies, their suits expressing individual wealth and splendour. The more regimented clothing we now associate with the royal gentlemen presents a less frivolous and ostentatious image.

Prince Andrew, was attired in his ceremonial day-dress uniform as a Lieutenant in the Royal Navy – with two bands of gold lace on the cuffs indicating his rank. As an ADC to the Queen, his aiguillette was worn, like Prince Charles, over his right shoulder. In addition to the neck-badge of the Commander of the Royal Victorian Order, he had on his chest the campaign medal for the South Atlantic (Falklands) War, together with the Jubilee Medal.

The Prince of Wales wore his full-dress commander's uniform, with the Stars of Orders of Garter and Thistle, the neck Order of the Grand Master of the Order of the Bath and now, in addition to the Coronation and Jubilee Medals, he wore the Queen's Service Order of New Zealand.

Prince Philip wore the full-dress uniform of an admiral of the fleet and Prince Edward, then an acting Lieutenant in the Royal Marines, dressed in his Number One dress uniform. Captain Mark Phillips did not wear the scarlet full-dress made for him by Dege and Company for his wedding with Princess Anne; rather, he chose a dark blue Number One dress uniform. Interestingly, both Colonel Johnson of the Lord Chamberlain's Office, and Sir John Miller, the Crown Equerry, wore the full-dress of the Grenadier and Welsh Guards respectively. Was Captain Phillip's choice of the dark blue prompted by personal choice? Or was it felt that scarlet in the group photographs would be too prominent?

The strong naval theme was carried to the pages' costume, which exhibited a wealth of historical detail and diligent research by the maker, Gieves and Hawkes. Their costumes further explored the concept of history represented in dress – which is present in all full-dress uniform. Master Peter Phillips and Andrew Ferguson, the eldest of the four pages, wore midshipmens' uniforms in a style borrowed from the years between 1782 and 1789. This uniform would not have been out of place at

ABOVE: *The newly married Duke and Duchess of York greeting the crowds of spectators after their wedding in Westminster Abbey. (Syndication International)*

OPPOSITE PAGE: *Prince William, age four, in Victorian-style sailor suit, complete with regulation naval dirk. He amused himself throughout the ceremony by teasing Miss Laura Fellowes, a bridesmaid. (Syndication International)*

the wedding of one of Miss Ferguson's ancestors, Lord George Cavendish, who was married in 1782. The research was carried out by Robert Gieves, consulting – amongst other sources – the company's archive to ensure accuracy. His passion for detail extended to a mock 'pay', which he presented to the pages – the equivalent of one day's wages, appropriate to the ranks of the pages and bearing the correct dates. The midshipmen, therefore, received a sixpence, and the two younger pages, dressed in sailor suits, a groat.

The midshipman's coat was of blue cloth, with nine gilt buttons down the front. There were no lapels and the coat was correctly lined with white cloth. The white waistcoat was single-breasted and the breeches of the same colour fastened at the knee with gilt buttons. At the neck was a white lace jabot and a black silk handkerchief. White hose, or stockings, and black shoes with a gilt buckle completed the outfit. Even the buttons had the correct fouled anchor device carefully engraved upon them.

The younger pages, Prince William and Seamus Makim, were in sailor suits, a child's costume familiar to many, but in this case derived from the prototype. When Queen Victoria's son Prince Albert Edward, then aged five, was cruising onboard the royal yacht *Victoria and Albert* during the summer of 1846, a member of the crew made him a costume based on the uniform worn by the crew. It was this costume that formed the basis of the pages' dress. The top garment, known as a frock, was in white, with a blue band on the upper arm. There was a blue denim collar. The frock was tucked into white trousers, which were made with the correct fall front and not the modern fly. Under the frock was a striped shirt. A hat of bleached Panama grass, with a broad brim and a shallow crown, was trimmed with a black ribbon, which fell in long tails at the back. Because Albert Edward wore a small seaman's knife at the time, both young pages were provided with a similar knife, to be carried at the waist.

After the wedding, the Duke and Duchess of York – the dukedom bestowed upon Prince Andrew on the eve of the wedding – drove to Buckingham Palace in the 1902 State landau, followed by the Queen and Major Ronald Ferguson in the semi-State landau. Following the wedding breakfast – and the obligatory appearance and kiss on the balcony of Buckingham Palace – the Duchess changed into her going-away outfit, a white silk *crêpe de chine* dress with a blue and green pattern. Accompanied by the Duke and a large teddy bear, she left in a coach, showered by thousands of rose petals thrown by the royal family and their household staff.

When the Prince and Princess of Wales married in 1981, one commentator recalled the judgement that a sociologist had expounded at the time of the marriage of Princess Elizabeth. 'There can be no society,' he had written, 'which does not feel the need of upholding and reaffirming at regular intervals the collective sentiments and collective ideas that make up its unity and personality.' Royal marriages achieve this. But a simpler and equally perceptive attitude to the function of royal weddings was summed up by the Duchess of York on the eve of her wedding in 1986. Asked about the pomp and circumstance, she replied, 'Fantastic, the more the merrier. More carriages, more pomp, wonderful. I love it.'

Don't we all?